MUSIC IN EARLY LUTHERANISM

CONCORDIA ACADEMIC PRESS

MUSIC IN EARLY LUTHERANISM

SHAPING THE TRADITION (1524–1672)

CARL SCHALK

Concordia Academic Press
A Division of
Concordia Publishing House
Saint Louis, Missouri

Cover illustration: Taken from the discant part of Georg Rhau's *Symphoniae iucundae* (1538).

Copyright ©2001 Carl Schalk
Published by Concordia Academic Press, a division of Concordia Publishing House
3558 S. Jefferson Avenue, Saint Louis, MO 63118-3968
Manufactured in the United States of America

Library of Congress Cataloging-in-Publication Data

Schalk, Cark
  Music in early Lutheranism : shaping the tradition (1524-1672) / by Carl Schalk
    p. cm.
  ISBN 0-570-04279-8
  1. Church music—Lutheran Church—16th century. 2. Church music—Lutheran Church—17th century. 3. Church music—Germany—16th century. 4. Church music —Germany—17th century. 5. Church musicians—Germany. I. Title.
  ML3168 .S24 2000
  781.71′41′009031—dc21   00-52380

---

1 2 3 4 5 6 7 8 9 10   10 09 08 07 06 05 04 03 02 01

Dedicated to the memory
of Walter E. Buszin (1899–1973)
and Paul G. Bunjes (1914–98),
my teachers, my colleagues, and my friends

Contents

Illustrations

Preface

The first two centuries of the Lutheran Reformation—the period between Martin Luther and Johann Sebastian Bach—produced a singularly impressive body of music written specifically for the worship life of the church. Less often noted is that this music developed as a clear result of Lutheranism's understanding of worship and the important place it gave to the art form it considered next in importance to theology. To explore the music of Lutheranism's early years is to see most clearly how what Lutherans thought about music in the life of the church was given shape and form in the actual music of those times.

The attention and acclaim properly given to Bach as the culminating figure of Lutheran church music in the 18th century have tended to overshadow the significance of those earlier generations of composers who, in the first 150 years of the Reformation, set the course Lutheran music was to follow. This brief study focuses on the life, work, and significance of seven church musicians who lived and worked in the first century-and-a-half of Lutheranism's evolvement and who were of great importance in the early development of the Lutheran tradition of music: Johann Walter (1496–1570), Georg Rhau (1488–1548), Hans Leo Hassler (1564–1612), Michael Praetorius (1571–1621), Johann Hermann Schein (1586–1630), Samuel Scheidt (1587–1654), and Heinrich Schuetz (1585–1672). The somewhat arbitrary parameters of this study are set by the publication in 1524 of the *Geystliche gesangk Buchleyn* of Johann Walter and the death of Heinrich Schuetz in 1672, a period of time just two years short of a century-and-a-half. This survey is an attempt to sketch briefly those first 150 years and to bring into somewhat clearer focus the significance of the work done by these pioneer church musicians.

To some the names of these seven early Lutheran church musicians may be largely unknown. To others they may be known only by name or through a passing acquaintance with a particular composition. Yet these are the men in whose music the evangelical thrust of the Reformation took shape to combine a truly popular vehicle of the people—the chorale—with art music of the highest degree of excellence. The result of their efforts was some of the greatest church music the world has ever known.

This brief introduction to early Lutheran music focuses on the musicians and musical developments of the early Reformation years as they reflected the church's understanding of music's place in its life and worship as seen through the musical works of the men who shaped Lutheran music's early course. Such a survey should help contribute to a better understanding of the roots of Lutheran music. It should also help to correct and clarify distortions and misunderstandings about the role of music in Lutheran worship, distortions and misunderstandings not uncommon even today.

In addition to the biographical information about each of these men, a discussion of their principal works, and the significance of their contribution in the musical world of their day, each section also includes selected references for further reading and study with the emphasis on materials available in English whenever possible. The collected works of each composer, as far as they are presently available, are listed in a manner that the reader may conveniently find particular works.

It is certainly true—and particularly unfortunate—that the music of these early Lutheran composers has largely fallen into eclipse and that one rarely hears this music in the public worship of Lutheran congregations today. This may be because of the general lack of availability of this material in editions practical for congregational usage and in part because of the changes in the musical tastes of succeeding generations. But perhaps most important of all, it may be a silent testimony to the degree to which we in our day have moved away from the theological and liturgical understandings, motivations, and foundations which helped to shape Lutheran music in the 16th and 17th centuries.

To call for a fresh look at the theological ideas which motivated these early Lutheran composers and which served as an inspiration to their craft of composition need not be viewed, as some might have it, as a simple, naive repristination of archaic ideas. Nor need the attempt to recover much of this music for worship today be seen simply as an anachronistic, backward-looking romanticism. Rather, to examine more closely the music of early Lutheranism together with the theological ideas which motivated its composers may well be the first step to approaching more realistically and faithfully the problems and questions which continue to vex the musical and liturgical life of today's church. It may well be the first step toward the recovery of music for worship and the liturgy that—in the early Reformation years—was seen as vital, exciting, and faithful to the challenge of praise and proclamation. A more thorough acquaintance with both the theology and the music of that time may well serve a similar role in our own day.

Carl Schalk
Concordia University
River Forest, Illinois

SHAPERS OF THE TRADITION

1480 1500 1520 1540 1560 1580 1600 1620 1640 1660 1680

Martin Luther (1483–1546)

Johann Walter (1496–1570)

Georg Rhau (1488–1548)

Hans Leo Hassler (1564–1612)

Michael Praetorius (1571–1621)

Johann Hermann Schein (1586–1630)

Samuel Scheidt (1587–1654)

Heinrich Schuetz (1585–1672)

1

The Context of the Reformation

From Renaissance to Baroque

Any introduction to the music of the early years of the Reformation era must necessarily take into account the theological and musical context in which the events of the period occurred. First and foremost is Martin Luther himself. It is difficult, if not impossible, to overestimate the importance of this central figure of the Reformation and his impact on the music and worship life of the Reformation church. But of equal importance were such other factors as the impact of the movement toward the use of the vernacular, the continuity of liturgical forms and musical practices which the Reformation encouraged, the impact of these factors on the music of the liturgy, and the consequences of the larger musical developments of the time as the church—together with the larger culture—moved out of the Renaissance and into the Baroque period.

Martin Luther (1483–1546)

Martin Luther was hardly a musical dilettante. Paul Henry Lang speaks of Luther in the following glowing terms:

> In the center of the new musical movement which accompanied the Reformation stands the great figure of Martin Luther . . . who, as a student in Eisenach singing all sorts of merry student songs, and as a celebrant priest familiar with the gradual and the polyphonic Masses and motets, lived with music ringing in his ears.[1]

It was Martin Luther who alone among the 16th-century reformers diligently and enthusiastically fostered the use of music in worship.[2] In contrast to both Ulrich Zwingli (1484–1531), who allowed no music of any kind in his services, and John Calvin (1509–64), who would have none of the art and artifice of music in worship except for unaccompanied congregational song, Luther encouraged the most sophisticated music of

---

[1] Paul Henry Lang, *Music in Western Civilization* (New York: W. W. Norton & Co., 1941), 207.

[2] For an introduction to Luther's thoughts on music in the church, see Carl Schalk, *Luther on Music: Paradigms of Praise* (St. Louis: Concordia, 1988).

his time—Gregorian chant and classical polyphony—together with the simpler congregational song of the chorale. Luther would have none of Augustine's qualms concerning music in worship, about which he commented:

> St. Augustine was afflicted with scruples of conscience whenever he discovered that he had derived pleasure from music and had been made happy thereby; he was of the opinion that such joy is unrighteous and sinful. He was a fine pious man; however, if he were living today, he would hold with us . . .[3]

Luther, rather than follow Augustine's thinking, encouraged instead a lively nurture and use of this art for the glory of God and the proclamation of His Word.

Luther was an accomplished musician, a singer, and a player of the lute. He had come to love the richness and splendor of Gregorian chant throughout his education and especially in his service as a priest. The great polyphonic music of the time was part of his cultural heritage, and he was acquainted with at least some of the great music and musical figures of his day. Simply to have set all this aside was, for Luther, neither possible nor desirable.

At the heart of Luther's concern was his view of music as a gift of God to be nurtured and used by man for his delight and edification, as a means for giving praise to the Creator, and as a vehicle for the proclamation of God's Word. It was God's gift to man to be used for God's purposes. There was no contradiction between speech and music because to "say and sing" was, for Luther, a single concept resulting from the inevitable eruption of joyful song in the heart and life of the redeemed.[4]

The content of that proclamation was, for Luther, clear and unambiguous: the good news of the Gospel. The Gospel determined the self-identity of the Christian community; if the community's proclamation was something other than the Gospel, it ceased to be a *Christian* community. To speak of music as *viva vox evangelii* ("living voice of the Gospel") was to state unequivocally that for the song to be "living," the

---

[3] Translated by Walter E. Buszin and quoted from the Erlangen edition of *Luther's Works,* LXII, 111.

[4] Nowhere is this seen more clearly than in Luther's Christmas hymn: "From heaven above to earth I come / To bear good news to every home; / Glad tidings of great joy I bring, / Whereof I now will say and sing" (*The Lutheran Hymnal* 85). The original German text is "Davon ich sing'n und sagen will." This nuance has been lost in some recent translations. See also the "Preface to the Babst Hymnal" (1545), *Luther's Works* (eds. J. Pelikan and H. T. Lehmann; St. Louis and Philadelphia, 1955–86), 53:333. (Hereafter *LW.*)

content of the song must be the Gospel. It was in the proclamation of the Gospel that God was truly praised and mankind truly edified. For Luther, music was the vehicle for that doxological proclamation—proclaimed both to the world as "good news" and to God, praising Him for it and pleading it before Him. The chief—though certainly not the only—locus for its proclamation was the liturgy.

In stressing the idea of the royal priesthood of all believers, Luther laid the foundation for the involvement of every Christian in corporate proclamation and praise at the highest level of each individual's ability. In emphasizing the understanding that all music falls under God's redemptive hand, Luther affirmed the freedom of the Christian to use all of music in praise of God and in the proclamation of the Gospel.

Luther's ideas gave strong direction and focus to the use of music in Lutheran worship. On the basis of these views the church musicians of the time developed a living tradition in which both simple congregational song and the art music of the time found a comfortable and appropriate place. The result was an outpouring of music which has few parallels in the history of church music.

The Impact of the Vernacular

The Lutheran Reformation is closely allied with the idea of worship in the vernacular. Luther was concerned that worship be understood by the people and that all could participate in their own tongue. The initial thrust toward the vernacular in early Lutheran worship is seen most clearly in the introduction of vernacular hymns and chorales. As early as 1523, Luther expressed the wish that "we had as many songs as possible in the vernacular which the people could sing during mass."[5] His encouragement to poets to produce psalms and hymns in the language of the people is well known, and the years that followed saw the production of a body of hymnody of unusual strength and quality.

Yet in his *Deudsche Messe und ordnung Gottis diensts* (*The German Mass and Order of Service,* 1526), Luther clearly expressed himself that "in no wise would I want to discontinue the service in the Latin language" and that "I do not agree with those who cling to one language and despise all others."[6] His first order of worship was in fact a Latin order, the *Formula Missae et Communionis pro Ecclesia Vuittembergensi* (*An Order of Mass and Communion for the Church at Wittenberg,* 1523), produced for the church at Wittenberg. In his writings on worship, Luther made clear that neither of his published orders was to be imposed on Lutheran

---

[5] *LW* 53:36.

[6] *LW* 53:63.

parishes; they were descriptive of his views and not to be made prescriptive. Nor was the *Deudsche Messe* in some sense to supercede or replace his earlier *Formula Missae* as a product of his more fully developed thought. Where Latin was understood—in the Latin schools and in the universities and larger towns—the basic Latin Mass should continue. The *Deudsche Messe*, on the other hand, was designed for the smaller towns and villages where Latin was not understood. In actual practice, these orders—the Latin Mass (1523) and the German Mass (1526)—were the poles between which Lutheran worship in the 16th century worked its way, many of the different *Kirchenordnungen* in the 16th century employing elements from both of Luther's orders.[7]

That Latin continued to be used in many places and in a variety of ways is evident from the many collections of Latin motets, setting of Ordinary and Proper texts of the Mass in Latin, as well as Latin responsories and canticles which continued to be published throughout the 16th century by the most prominent Lutheran composers. Georg Rhau's various publications, intended for use in Lutheran worship, are striking cases in point.

While the use of the vernacular continued to increase as the Reformation spread throughout Germany and the Scandinavian countries, it is interesting to note that as late as the time of Bach the churches in Leipzig continued to hear polyphonic motets in Latin, Latin Glorias, chanted Latin Collects, and the Creed sung in Latin by the choir, as well as other portions of the service. While the simultaneous juxtaposition of German and Latin in 16th-century Lutheran worship may be viewed as a paradox, it may also be seen as further evidence of that freedom and catholicity which characterized much of Lutheran worship at that time.

The Continuity of Liturgical Forms and Practices

Luther's view of music was entirely consonant with his understanding of the relationship between the church's worship and its traditional worship forms and piety. Simply stated, Luther's approach was to retain from the past whatever did not violate his understanding of the Gospel. This was no flight into a wistful nostalgia, but rather a pastorally responsible attempt to demonstrate the continuity and unity of Lutheranism with the church catholic.

Thus any view of Luther as a radical liturgical reformer is fundamen-

---

[7] See, for example, Friedrich Blume, *Protestant Church Music: A History* (New York: W. W. Norton & Co., 1974), 51 ff. Also Robin Leaver, "Christian Liturgical Music in the Wake of the Protestant Reformation," in *Sacred Sound and Social Change: Liturgical Music in Jewish and Christian Experience* (Notre Dame: University of Notre Dame Press, 1992), 124–44.

tally mistaken. While certain new emphases did indeed characterize Luther's reforms—the importance of the sermon, communion in both kinds, the use of vernacular congregational song as an integral part of the liturgy—what is striking about Luther's approach is its basic conservatism. In his Latin Mass of 1523, Luther could state unequivocally that

> It is not now nor ever has been our intention to abolish the liturgical service of God . . . [8]

And in "Receiving Both Kinds in the Sacrament," he remarked:

> Let the old practice continue. Let the mass be celebrated with consecrated vestments, with chants and all the usual ceremonies, in Latin . . . [9]

Even a cursory examination of the various Lutheran orders from the 16th century clearly demonstrates that the general outline of the medieval orders was deliberately carried into the Lutheran practice of the time. Luther saw no need to reject out of hand worship structures which in their richness of Scripture and splendor of their music were still viable vehicles for the praise of God. Only when specific texts or practices reflected a misunderstanding of the thrust of the Gospel did Luther feel constrained to alter and change. (His excising of the Canon of the Mass is the most notable example.)

Whether in the Mass or the Canonical Hours (which Luther reduced to two, Matins and Vespers, to meet more realistically the situation in parish churches), the general structure of the medieval forms remained essentially intact in 16th-century Lutheranism. Nothing could be more eloquent testimony to the fact that Luther saw his reforms not as the unilaterally instituted ideas of an individual, but rather as a reform within the church catholic that sought to demonstrate whenever possible the continuity between itself and the whole history of Christian worship and piety.

The importance for the 16th-century church musician of such continuity of liturgical forms and practices was self-evident. For the most part, music useful or necessary in Catholic worship continued to be useful in the reformed church. With the exception of the chorale and the music that developed around it, there was, in fact, little difference between the music used in Catholic and Lutheran worshiping communities in the 16th century. Polyphonic settings of the Ordinary and Proper texts for the church year, antiphons, responsories, hymns based on the old church melodies, canticles, motets on biblical texts—all these were common building blocks for church musicians in both Lutheran and Catholic communities

[8] *LW* 53:20.
[9] *LW* 36:254.

during this time. The music held in common in Lutheran and Catholic worship of the period was a striking example of such liturgical continuity.

From Renaissance . . .

The music of the early Lutheran Reformation was the music of the Renaissance. While such a statement may seem simply to be repeating the obvious, it needs to be repeated because music of this time is hardly a well-known musical language in today's worshiping communities. Its absence from the repertoire of most church choirs in the 20th century hardly helps us to experience and understand the sounds with which Luther grew up and which constituted the basic musical idiom of Lutheranism's first half-century. The music of the Renaissance remained the basic musical vocabulary of Lutheranism until the time when a new musical language, developing in Italy, would begin to find its way to Germany in the latter 1500s.

The Flemish School

Josquin Desprez (1440–1521), undoubtedly the greatest of the Renaissance masters, and to a lesser extent Heinrich Isaac (ca. 1450–1517), court composer to Maximillian I, emperor of the Holy Roman Empire (1493–1519), dominated the music of the early 1500s. Both were part of that general development which music historians refer to as the "Flemish" or "Netherlands" school, so named because of the association of many of the important composers of the time with the Netherlands and the emigration of many of them to other European countries where they held important posts in chapels and at various courts. Both Josquin and Isaac were inheritors of the great tradition of the intricate polyphony and technical ingenuity of such earlier Netherlands masters as Ockeghem (ca. 1420–96) and Obrecht (1450/1–1505).

The Flemish school was the most influential movement in the music of the Renaissance, its influence covering the period from about 1450–1600 when new stylistic developments would turn the history of music in new directions. Among the chief characteristics of the Flemish school was the use of a polyphonic style in which all of the parts were generally of equal importance and in which imitation was the chief means to establish that equality. The style was characterized by a clear texture, smooth-sounding polyphony and homophony, controlled expressiveness, and well-organized principles of composition, including a controlled use of dissonance and consonance.

It was the music of the Flemish school that Luther knew well and about which he frequently spoke. He particularly expressed fondness and appreciation for the music of Josquin, about whom he remarked:

> Josquin is a master of the notes, which must express what he desires; on the other hand, other choral composers must do what the notes dictate.[10]

> God has preached the Gospel through music, too, as may be seen in Josquin, all of whose compositions flow freely, gently, and cheerfully, are not forced or cramped by rules, and are like the song of the finch.[11]

Luther's various comments about music, whether in his more informal remarks collected in his "table talk" or in the more formal prefaces to the various publications for which he provided introductions, must always be interpreted in light of the prevailing musical style of his time, that of Flemish polyphony. This was the music with which he grew up, the music he loved, the music which from his earliest years, as Paul Henry Lang has remarked, was "ringing in his ears."

Voices and Instruments

In general, there was little or no distinction between vocal and instrumental styles of writing in the 16th century. Music could be performed by voices or instruments or by various combinations of both. Instruments in common use included recorders, shawms, crumhorns, cornetts, trumpets, trombones, viols, and lutes in a variety of sizes and pitch levels. In addition, there was a gradual tendency to move from mixed consorts of instruments to the use of sets or families of similar instruments, which provided a uniform timbre throughout the entire range. Vocal polyphonic music of the Renaissance was sometimes accompanied either by the organ or other instruments, the instruments simply doubling the voice parts—or some of them. Vocal music of the time was often transcribed for keyboard and other instruments, and ornamentation or elaboration of various kinds was sometimes written out and sometimes improvised by the performers.

Vocal music was not written out in full score nor did it include bar lines. Usually it was either set out in choirbook arrangement, in which the various parts were notated separately on one or two pages of a large open book set on a large stand around which the singers would gather, or—with increasing frequency—in partbooks in which each book contained only the music for a single voice. Choirs were generally small—a normal 16th-century choir often consisting of no more than 12 to 16 singers, often

---

[10] M. Johann Mathesius, *Dr. Martin Luthers Leben* (St. Louis, 1883), 227 f.; quoted in Walter E. Buszin, *Luther on Music*, Pamphlet Series, no. 3 (ed. Johannes Riedel; St. Paul: Lutheran Society for Worship, Music and the Arts, 1958), 13.

[11] *LW* 54:129–30.

fewer. Frequently the composer would only set out the initial words beneath the notes, leaving the fitting of the remaining words to the music up to the singers.

Music and the Liturgy

For the most part, Lutheran choirs—where they existed—participated within the structure of the liturgy. Polyphonic settings of the Ordinary of the Mass (Kyrie, Gloria, Credo, Sanctus, Agnus Dei) and certain of the Proper texts continued to be written for the Lutheran service throughout the 16th century and beyond. Antiphons, psalms, hymns, and other portions of Matins and Vespers continued to be set to music by such composers as Walter, Hassler, and Praetorius, or older settings by Catholic composers were used as they were found in any of several collections made available for use in Lutheran worship. Settings for the liturgy continued to be written in both Latin and German languages throughout the 16th and 17th centuries. It will be helpful for the reader to have an acquaintance with the early Lutheran liturgical orders, which essentially continued the late medieval structure of the Catholic Mass. (See Appendix A.) Without such an acquaintance, any discussion of the role of music in those structures will prove difficult to understand.

For Luther, church music was essentially limited to vocal polyphony, Gregorian chant, and Latin and vernacular hymnody. Nowhere does he seem to recognize the organ as capable of making any significant contribution to worship. Yet the organ did function in early Lutheran worship— as any survey of the various church orders of the time indicates. The organ provided intonations and alternate verses for such portions of the liturgy as the Introit, Gloria in Excelsis, sequence hymns, responsories, and for such canticles as the Magnificat and Te Deum.[12] The use of the organ to accompany congregational singing of the hymns and chorales as we generally experience it today was unknown throughout the 16th century.

It was in the singing of the vernacular hymns and chorales that the congregation assumed a new importance in Lutheran worship. These vernacular hymns were de facto a part of the liturgy, and they provided the way for the people to sing the various parts of the liturgy in versified form. A common practice was for the congregation, choir, and sometimes the organ to alternate in the singing of a chorale. The congregation sang its stanzas in unison, unaccompanied, while the stanzas sung by the choir or those "sung" by the organ were presented in any of the many polyphonic settings which were written for just this purpose. This *alternatim praxis*

---

[12] See Herbert Gotsch, "The Organ in the Lutheran Service of the 16th Century," *Church Music* 67.1 (1967): 7–12.

(alternation practice)—with its roots in the practice of Gregorian chant—enabled the congregation to sing chorales of many stanzas without taxing any one group. To conceive of Lutheran hymnody as functioning in any other way in these early years is to misunderstand the role and function of hymnody in early Lutheran worship.

To summarize, the liturgical structure of early Lutheran worship and that of 16th-century Catholicism were, in large measure, similar. The music of the choir heard in both worshiping communities stood squarely in the Renaissance tradition of Flemish vocal polyphony. It was particularly in the music that developed around the singing of the vernacular chorale that Lutheranism reflected its uniqueness in those early years. This largely overlooked fact is crucial to a clearer understanding of the developments which were to occur as Lutheranism moved into the 17th century and beyond. It is to those developments that we now turn.

. . . to Baroque

By the end of the 16th century, new breezes from Italy were blowing across the musical landscape. They heralded a new period in the history of church music which would last for at least a century and a half. What we call the Renaissance was drawing to a close; what we name as the Baroque period was just ahead. For example, the latter years of the 1500s saw a group of progressive musicians in Venice pursuing a variety of innovative musical ideas. These included a polychoral style which contrasted a variety of high, low, or similar choirs, with and without instruments, placed in various parts of the church building; a progressive use of instruments used in a more idiomatic manner; experimentation with a variety of "echo" effects; and the aurally sensuous effect of the use of broad masses of sound. These efforts—associated with the names of Adrian Willaert (ca. 1490–1562) and his pupil Andrea Gabrieli (ca. 1510–86) and his pupil and nephew Giovanni Gabrieli (ca. 1553/56–1612)—were harbingers of music of a more dramatic and sensory nature than anything before it.

The Disintegration of Stylistic Unity

The most apparent effect of the new musical innovations emanating from Italy in the late 1500s, culminating about 1750 in the work of Bach, was the disintegration of the stylistic unity which had characterized the Renaissance. The disintegration of the Renaissance concept of the equality of all the parts in a musical texture gave way to the growing importance of the outer parts of the texture, the bass and soprano—in that order—finally assuming the greatest importance. The emergence of the *basso continuo,* or figured bass, as one of the most obvious characteristics

of Baroque musical style is evidence of this shift. This shift was supported, and in part assisted, by a freer use of dissonance and by the simultaneous movement toward a more harmonically oriented musical texture.

At the same time, the old system of modes, the basis for the music of
the Renaissance, slowly gave way to a tonal system oriented to
major/minor thinking. A comparison of the melodic and harmonic treatment of the 16th-century chorale melodies from Walter's *Geystliche
gesangk Buchleyn* (1524) through Michael Praetorius' *Musae Sioniae*
(1605–10) to the chorale harmonizations of Bach more than a hundred
years later clearly reflects this shift.

All of this opened the way for a freer treatment of melody far beyond
the restrictions of the smaller melodic intervals which were the mainstay
of Renaissance music. This, together with an approach to rhythm which
replaced the *tactus*—the basis for rhythmic organization in the
Renaissance—with a much freer treatment of rhythm, expanded the possibilities for a more subjective and dramatic declamation of the text. It
was the call for more dramatic textual declamation, particularly in relation to the solo voice, which was a significant factor that gave impetus to
a reorientation of thinking about rhythm. It was in the Baroque period, it
must be remembered, that the possibilities of the solo voice for the purpose of solo—as opposed to choral—song were first systematically
explored.

Perhaps the most dramatic effect of the disintegration of the stylistic
unity of the Renaissance was the fact that with the increasing adoption of
various innovative musical techniques, the composer now had to con-
sciously distinguish and choose between composing in the "old style"
(*prima prattica*) or the "new style" (*secunda prattica*). While Walter and
Rhau—the first two among the composers treated here—lived too early to
have been touched by these developments, Hassler, Praetorius, Schein,
Scheidt, and Schuetz all reflect, in varying degrees, the use of both "old"
and "new" styles.

The results of experimentation with these new techniques and devices
of the Baroque period inevitably found their way into the church music of
the time. Some composers traveled to Italy to learn firsthand from such
composers as Giovanni Gabrieli or Claudio Monteverdi—Hans Leo
Hassler and Heinrich Schuetz among them. Others availed themselves of
the printed editions of music which were available in increasing number.
Whatever the route, these new musical ideas were to have a profound
effect on Lutheran church music and would soon turn that music into new
paths significantly different in style and spirit from that about which
Luther spoke.

Pietism and the "New Style"

This new music presented the church with an interesting challenge. As long as the church continued to use music in the older polyphonic style, the statements of Luther spoken in the context of that musical style could continue to be used in support of such music in the worship life of the church. But with the radical change in the musical situation in the 17th century, descriptions of music such as the following by Luther were increasingly out of touch with the actual music of the time.

> Here it is most remarkable that one single voice continues to sing the tenor, while at the same time many other voices play around it, exulting and adorning it in exuberant strains and, as it were, leading it forth in a divine roundelay, so that those who are the least bit moved know nothing more amazing in this world.[13]

Such a word picture perfectly describes a Josquin *cantus-firmus* motet, as well as Luther's own modest attempt to set one of his favorite passages to music[14] (Ex. 1). But one could hardly expect such a statement to be readily understood when applied to music which was no longer linear and contrapuntal but increasingly vertical, largely homophonic, and probably not even based on a *cantus firmus*.

Ex. 1. Martin Luther, "Non moriar sed vivam"

What many Lutheran theologians did during the latter years of the 16th and the early years of the 17th century was, for the most part, to continue

---

[13] *LW* 53:324. From the preface to Georg Rhau's *Symphoniae iucundae*.

[14] This four-part *cantus-firmus* motet was published under Luther's name in the drama *Lazarus* by Joachim Greff (Wittenberg, 1545) and is generally credited to Luther. The *cantus firmus*, found in the tenor part as was customary, is the eighth psalm tone in the florid canticle version. A transcription of this motet with English text (the text "Non moriar sed vivam" ["I shall not die but live"] was known to be a favorite of Luther) is found in *LW* 53:339–41.

to repeat Luther's ideas and concepts, quite oblivious to the fact that they were less and less applicable to the actual music of their day. While Luther's remarks made frequent reference to the actual music of his day, one searches in vain for similar remarks in the statements of the 17th-century apologists of orthodoxy. Furthermore, as Lutheranism moved through the 1600s and into the 1700s, the course charted by a developing Pietism was to retreat from Luther's joyous exuberance and delight in all of music to a more solemn and somber view. Pietism tended to identify the "new style" as essentially secular and, therefore, unsuited for worship, full of the dangers of theatricality and concertizing.[15]

Typical of the reaction of a nascent Pietism, though spoken from within the camp of orthodoxy, are the comments of Theophil Grossgebauer (1627–61), who complained:

> . . . alas, organists, choirmasters, flutists, and other musicians, many of them unspiritual people, rule in our city churches. They play and sing, fiddle and bow to their hearts' content. You hear the various noises but do not know what they mean . . . One chases the other in their concertizing manner, and they contend in rivalry to see who can perform most artistically and come closest to the nightingale.[16]

From the same context comes the comment of Johann Konrad Dannhauer (1630–66), orthodox theologian and teacher of Spener, whose concern that the words not be overshadowed by the music reflects a common complaint of this more privatistic view of edification.

> The simple human voice is doubtless sweeter than any lifeless pipe or string; but the pipe overwhelms it, the string drowns it, so that it can scarcely be heard. It is useless and fruitless, for it obscures the sense of the song so that the church cannot know what is being sung and cannot respond with Amen.[17]

Even Bach, some years later, was not exempt from such criticism. His troubles with the Pietists are well known. In Arnstadt, where the simpler style was apparently preferred by the Pietists and where Bach served from 1703–7, he was reproved for the many curious *variationes* in the chorale

---

[15] For a general introduction to Lutheran thinking about worship and music in the 17th century, see Friedrich Kalb, *Theology of Worship in 17th-Century Lutheranism* (St. Louis: Concordia, 1965). A more recent treatment is Joyce L. Irwin, *Neither Voice nor Heart Alone: German Lutheran Theology of Music in the Age of the Baroque,* vol. 132 of *Series VII: Theology and Religion,* American University Studies (New York: Peter Lang, 1993).

[16] Quoted in Friedrich Kalb, *Theology of Worship in 17th-Century Lutheranism* (St. Louis: Concordia, 1965), 145.

[17] Ibid., 145.

that mingled many strange tones and for the fact that the congregation was confused by it.[18]

Bach was also criticized by Johann Mattheson for his frequent repetition of words, a device which Mattheson felt only obscured the meaning of the text. Christian Gerber's 1732 description of Passion music of the time, while most likely not referring to Bach's *St. Matthew Passion,* is, nevertheless, particularly reflective of the view of 18th-century Pietism.

> In the pew of a noble family in church, many . . . were present who sang the first Passion chorale out of their books with great devotion. But when this theatrical music began, all these people were thrown into the greatest bewilderment. . . . It's just as if one were at an Opera Comedy. But everyone was genuinely displeased by it and voiced just complaints against it. There are, it is true, some people who take pleasure in such idle things, especially if they are of a sanguine temperament and inclined to sensual pleasure. Such persons defend large-scale church compositions as best they can . . .[19]

Lutheran Pietism chose to prefer a more simple, solemn musical style which it felt was better suited to its largely personal and privatistic concept of edification. Such a view—where it was dominant—was effected at the cost of a rupture with the general musical culture of its time. Thus in the Baroque period, a period highly receptive to the cultivation of the arts, Lutheran Pietism advocated a fundamentally reactionary rejection of what it considered to be a secular intrusion into the musical life of the church. This was the logical consequence of Pietism's failure to come to terms with Luther's more basic understandings of theology and music and for failing to advance those ideas in ways which could more adequately come to terms with what was a new musical situation.

What musicians such as Hassler, Praetorius, Schein, Scheidt, and Schuetz did was to assimilate into their own work, in a variety of ways, the approach and devices of the Baroque period and to connect them with the two basic sources of Lutheran musical identity: the liturgy and the chorale. In so doing, they were acting in a manner faithful to Luther's concept of music as God's gift to be nourished and used for the edification of God's people and for the proclamation of the Word. In so doing, they were also being faithful to their craft and proved to be men of their own time.

While this philosophy was nowhere developed systematically by these men, one catches elements of it in some of their writings and in some of

---

[18] Hans T. David and Arthur Mendel, eds., revised and expanded by Christoph Wolff, *The New Bach Reader: A Life of Johann Sebastian Bach in Letters and Documents* (New York: W. W. Norton & Co., 1998), 46.

[19] Ibid., 325–27.

the prefaces to their work. That such was indeed their philosophy is most clearly seen in their music, which, while retaining important and crucial ties to Lutheranism's theological and musical tradition, nevertheless refused to be bound by the parameters of another time and age. These men remained open to the musical culture of the day and produced—in faithfulness to the essence of Luther's thought—some of the greatest music in the history of the church.

Johann Walter

First Cantor of the Lutheran Church

Johann Walter (1496–1570) occupies a unique position in the musical history of the Reformation. As the first Lutheran cantor, as friend and advisor to Martin Luther, and as a composer of a wide variety of liturgical music for the needs of the Reformation church and its Latin schools, Walter occupies a pivotal position at the beginning of the development of Lutheran church music, a development which was to culminate in a singular way—some two hundred years later—in the music of Johann Sebastian Bach.

As part of his vocation as a musician serving the church, Walter was also concerned with a proper theological understanding of the use of music in the life and worship of the Christian community. Next to Luther himself, Walter occupies a special place in the establishment of the Reformation's outlook on the role of music in Christian life and worship. His *Lob und Preis der loeblichen Kunst Musica* (*In Praise of the Noble Art of Music*)—a rhymed didactic poem of 324 lines written in 1538 in which he develops an entire theology of music based on Reformation insights—is a unique document in the history of the music of the Reformation. In many ways it surpasses even Luther's "Vorrhede auff alle gute Gesangbuecher" ("A Preface for All Good Hymnals"), which Luther wrote as an introduction to Walter's poem.

Walter's ideas about music in the life of the church, as well as his music itself, deserve to be better known. This brief sketch is intended to serve as an introduction to his life, his thought, and his music.[1]

Johann Walter (Walther) was born in Kahla on the Thuringian Saale near Jena in central Germany in 1496. The details of his early life are not entirely clear. A supplement to his will dated April 1, 1562, suggests that his name was Blankenmueller and that he was adopted by a citizen of Kahla named Walter.[2] It is just as likely that his mother's name was Blankenmueller and that his father, Hans, was a prosperous farmer in the

---

[1] The material in this chapter is an expanded version of Carl Schalk, *Johann Walter: First Cantor of the Lutheran Church* (St. Louis: Concordia, 1992).

[2] See Wilhelm Ehmann, "Johann Walter. Der erste Kantor der Prot. Kirche," *Musik und Kirche* VI (1934): 188–203, 240–46.

region.[3] Whatever may have been the case, it is generally agreed that
Walter attended the Latin school in his native city of Kahla, where he also
served as a choirboy. Beyond this, little is known of his early life, especially where he received his musical education. It was not until he was to
enter the court of Frederick the Wise in 1517 that we hear further of
Walter. It was to be the beginning of a career which would place him at
the very center of musical life in the formative years of the Lutheran
Reformation.

Walter at Torgau (1517–48)

In 1517, at the instigation of Conrad Rupsch (ca. 1475–1530),
Hofkapellmeister at the court of Frederick the Wise, Elector of Saxony,
the 21-year-old Walter entered the court chapel of Frederick as a bass
singer and as a young composer.[4] Frederick the Wise, who was Elector
from 1486 until his death in 1525, made his court a center of musical and
artistic activity. Albrecht Duerer, Lucas Cranach the Elder, Peter Vischer
the Younger, and Hans Vischer were among the many artists patronized by
him. In addition to his musical and artistic interests, Frederick had also
amassed a large collection of religious relics for which he was famous.[5]
Conrad Rupsch,[6] Frederick's *Hofkapellmeister*, was the successor of
Adam Rener,[7] a singer and composer at the court of Frederick the Wise,

---

[3] See Wilibald Gurlitt, "Johann Walter u. die Musik der Reformationszeit,"
Lutherjahrbuch XV (1933): 1–112.

[4] Gustav Reese, *Music in the Renaissance* (rev. ed.; New York: W. W. Norton & Co.,
1959), 677, indicates that Walter sang in the court choir from 1517–26. Werner Braun,
"Walter, Johann," in vol. 20 of *The New Grove Dictionary of Music and Musicians* (ed.
Stanley Sadie; New York: Macmillan, 1980), 188–89, suggests that Walter may not have
begun his court service until 1521. At this time Frederick the Wise divided his residence
among Torgau, Altenburg, and Weimar.

[5] Roland Bainton, *Here I Stand* (New York: Abingdon-Cokesbury, 1950), 69, speaks
of Frederick the Wise as a man "who had devoted a lifetime to making Wittenberg the
Rome of Germany as a depository of sacred relics." For a detailed description of the
variety and number of these relics, see E. G. Schwiebert, *Luther and His Times* (St.
Louis: Concordia, 1950), 242 ff.

[6] Conrad Rupsch (ca. 1475–1530) was associated with the *Hofkapelle* before 1500,
though it is uncertain when he assumed the position of *Hofkapellmeister*. Sometime after
1520, he apparently fell under the influence of the Enthusiast Karlstadt, a fact which
may have had something to do with the declining interest of Frederick the Wise in his
Hofkapelle.

[7] Adam Rener (ca. 1485–1520) was a choirboy at the court of Maximillian I in 1498.
From 1507 until his death in 1517, Rener was in the service of Frederick the Wise,
Elector of Saxony. Georg Rhau published five Masses of Rener (1541, 1545) and various
other works. Eight Magnificats of Rener were also published in 1544.

who had held the position beginning in 1507. Rener, a friend of Heinrich Isaac,[8] was one of the most famous musicians of his day. Isaac and Rener served together at the court of Maximillian I. It was into such a promising position that the young Walter came, an environment which was to provide the context for his early contribution to the music of the Reformation as the first cantor and composer of the Lutheran church.

In 1524, while still a young man and assistant to Rupsch, Walter— apparently with the encouragement and under the guidance of Luther[9]— published his *Geystliche gesangk Buchleyn*, a unique collection of 43 pieces for three, four, and five voices arranged according to the church year. Thirty-eight pieces were in German, five in Latin. All but two of the pieces were *cantus-firmus* compositions with the melody in the tenor part. The contents were intended primarily for the church choirs, which were composed principally of boys and older students in the schools. The songs were "arranged in four parts[10] to give the young—who should at any rate be trained in music and other fine arts—something to wean them away from love ballads and carnal songs and to give them something of value in their place, thus combining the good with the pleasing, as is proper for youth."[11] It is interesting that this collection—with the intention that it be used in the schools and with Luther's comments directed particularly to the young people—appeared in the same year as Luther's famous appeal "To the Councilmen of All Cities in Germany That They Establish and Maintain Christian Schools" (1524).[12]

Published in five partbooks, subsequent editions or reprints of Walter's collection appeared in 1525, 1528, 1534, 1537, 1544, and 1551. In comparing the first and later editions of Walter's *Geystliche gesangk Buchleyn*, it is interesting to note that while the edition of 1524 contained only five compositions in Latin, by the last edition of 1551 the number of Latin pieces had grown to 47. Apparently this collection was the prototype of the Wittenberg hymnal for the laity published in 1525, the texts and melodies of both collections appearing in exactly the same order.

---

[8] Heinrich Isaac (ca. 1450–1517) was one of the chief Netherlands polyphonists. Isaac was in the service of Lorenzo de Medici from 1480–92 as organist and *maestro di capella*. After spending some years in Rome, Isaac was called to the court of Maximillian I at Vienna as *Symphonista regis*. From 1514 until his death, Isaac lived in Florence.

[9] In the preface to Walter's *Geystichle gesangk Buchleyn*, Luther says: "Therefore I, too, in order to make a start and to give an incentive to those who can do better, have with the help of others compiled several hymns . . ." *LW* 53:316.

[10] Twenty-nine pieces are in four parts, 12 in five parts, and two in three parts.

[11] From the preface, *LW* 53:316.

[12] See *LW* 45:347 ff.

The polyphonic settings of the *Geystliche gesangk Buchleyn* were typically in tenor *cantus-firmus* style as in Ex. 2, which is based on the melody "Komm, Gott Schoepfer," which was the German adaptation of the Gregorian "Veni Creator Spiritus." Walter's six-part motet "Christe, qui lux es et dies," which first appeared in the 1537 edition, is an example of Walter's great polyphonic skill with the *cantus firmus* in long notes in canon between the tenor and altus parts, the remaining four parts weaving their way while using the melodic material of the *cantus firmus* as the basis for their somewhat freer treatment, as in Ex. 3.

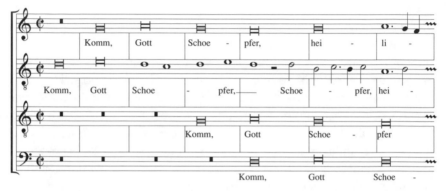

Ex. 2. Johann Walter, "Komm, Gott Schoepfer" from the *Geystliche gesangk Buchleyn*

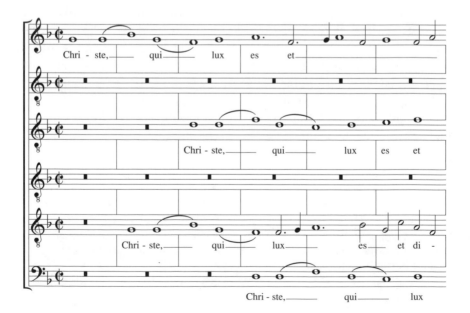

Ex. 3. Johann Walter, "Christe, qui lux es et dies" from the *Geystliche gesangk Buchleyn*

    Walter's treatment of the chorale melody may be seen in Ex. 4a and 4b. While the *cantus firmus* at this point in history would normally be found in the tenor part (as in Ex. 4a), occasionally, however, Walter would place the melody in the upper or discantus part (as in Ex. 4b), harbinger of a practice that would become the norm by the end of the 16th century.

Ex. 4a and 4b. Johann Walter, two settings from the *Geystliche gesangk Buchleyn*

    In addition to the polyphonic motet style, simple homophonic settings of the psalms and canticles, in tenor *cantus-firmus* style, are also found in Walter's work. The setting of the Nunc Dimittis (Ex. 5) for six voices is based on the eighth Gregorian tone found in the Tenor I part.

Nunc di - mit - tis ser-vum tu - um Do - mi - ne, se - cun-dum ver-bum tu - um, in pa - ce:

Nunc di - mit - tis ser-vum tu - um Do - mi - ne, se - cun-dum ver-bum tu - um, in pa - ce:

Nunc di - mit - tis ser-vum tu - um Do - mi - ne, se - cun-dum ver-bum tu - um, in pa - ce:

Nunc di - mit - tis ser-vum tu - um Do - mi - ne, se - cun-dum ver-bum tu - um, in pa - ce:

Nunc di - mit - tis ser-vum tu - um Do - mi - ne, se - cun-dum ver-bum tu - um, in pa - ce:

Nunc di - mit - tis ser-vum tu - um Do - mi - ne, se - cun-dum ver-bum tu - um, in pa - ce:

Ex. 5. Johann Walter, six-part setting of the Nunc Dimittis

Fig. 1. *The Ambassadors* by Hans Holbein the Younger, which shows the tenor partbook of the *Geystliche gesangk Buchleyn*

Walter's close contact and developing friendship with Martin Luther is already evident in this collection for which Luther provided the preface and in which Luther commended its use to young people and in general encouraged all the arts, and especially music, to be used "in the service of Him who gave and made them."[13] A unique indication of the renown of this collection is the depiction of two pages from the tenor partbook of the *Geystliche gesangk Buchleyn* in Hans Holbein the Younger's picture *The Ambassadors*.[14] The pages clearly show the melodies of "Komm, Heiliger Geist" and "Mensch, willst du leben seliglich." The same year in

---

[13] *LW* 53:316.

[14] Signed and dated 1533, the original is in the National Gallery in London. Hans Holbein the Younger was one of the greatest portrait painters of Europe. Born in Augsburg, the son of Hans Holbein the Elder, he eventually settled in London where this picture was painted.

which Walter published his *Geystliche gesangk Buchleyn* (1524), he also became the *Kapellmeister* in Torgau, the city in which he was to work for more than 30 years.

Walter also served, with Conrad Rupsch, as musical advisor to Luther in the preparation of Luther's *Deudsche Messe* (1526). Martin Luther, in the years following the publication of his *Formula Missae* (1523), devoted considerable attention to the preparation of a Mass in the vernacular. In 1524 Luther wrote that

> I would gladly have a German Mass today. I am also occupied with it. But I would very much like it to have a true German character. For to translate the Latin text and retain the Latin tone or notes has my sanction, although it doesn't sound polished or well done. Both the text and the notes, accent, melody, and manner of rendering ought to grow out of the mother tongue and its inflection, otherwise all of it becomes an imitation, in the manner of apes . . .[15]

Therefore, in 1525, Luther called for the assistance of Walter and Rupsch to help prepare the music for his German Mass. Later in his life, Walter, recalling his trip to Wittenberg, gave this description of the work.

> When he, Luther, forty years ago desired to introduce the German Mass in Wittenberg, he communicated this wish to the Prince Elector of Saxony and to the late Duke Johann. He urged his Electoral Highness to bring the old singing master, the worthy Konrad Rupsch, and me to Wittenberg. At that time he discussed with us the Gregorian chants and the nature of the eight modes, and finally he applied the eighth mode to the Epistle and the sixth mode to the Gospel, saying: "Christ is a kind Lord, and His words are sweet; therefore we want to take the sixth mode for the Gospel; and because Paul is a serious apostle we want to arrange the eighth mode for the Epistle." Luther himself wrote the music for the lessons and the words of institution of the true blood and body of Christ, sang them to me, and wanted to hear my opinion of it. He kept me for three weeks to note down properly the chants of the Gospels and Epistles, until the first mass was sung in Wittenberg. I had to attend it and take a copy of this first mass with me to Torgau. And one sees, hears, and understands at once how the Holy Spirit has been active not only in the authors who composed the Latin hymns and set them to music, but in Herr Luther himself, who now has invented most of the poetry and melody of the German chants. And it can be seen from the German Sanctus how he arranged all the notes to the text with the right accent and concent in masterly fashion. I, at the time, was tempted to ask His Reverence from where he had these pieces and his knowledge; whereupon the dear man laughed at my simplicity.

---

[15] *LW* 40:141.

He told me that the poet Virgil had taught him such, he, who is able so artistically to fit his meter and words to the story which he is narrating. All music should be so arranged that its notes are in harmony with the text.[16]

However, following the death of Elector Frederick the Wise in 1525 and the succession of John the Steadfast as Elector and Regent, the *Hofkapelle* in Torgau fell on bad times. Already in the last years of Frederick the Wise, there seemed to have been a declining interest on his part in the *Hofkapelle*. This may have been in part because Rupsch, in the years after 1520, had come under the influence of the Enthusiast Karlstadt. With the accession of John the Steadfast, the new Elector determined to disband the *Hofkapelle*. On June 20, 1526, Melanchthon wrote to John the Steadfast that he not put a man like Walter out of work because as Melanchthon said,

. . . he has composed songs that are sung a good deal at present. We have need of such people, not only in order that the good music that has been used might not be buried, but also that new and better music might be written. I consider retaining the services of such people a good work from which God derives pleasure. Thus far have people in many places maintained music groups for unnecessary pomp and other unbecoming purposes. Why should the noble art of music not remain active now for God's sake, since it is used for the service and glory of God.[17]

The same day, Luther also wrote to John the Steadfast on the same subject.

Finally, my most gracious Lord, I request again that Your Electoral Grace will not permit the *Kantorei* to pass out of existence, especially since those who are at present its members have been trained for such work; in addition, the art [of music] is worthy of being supported by Princes and Lords, much more so than many other endeavors and enterprises for which there is not nearly so much need. . . . The goods and possessions of the monasteries could well be used to take care of these people. God would derive pleasure from such a transfer.[18]

Such concern for Walter's future career was likely occasioned also by

---

[16] *Verba des alten Johann Walters* in Michael Praetorius' *Syntagma musicum I* (Wittenberg, 1614/15), 449–53. Quoted from Paul Nettl, *Luther on Music* (Philadelphia: Muhlenberg, 1948), 75–76.

[17] Quoted in Walter E. Buszin, *Luther on Music,* Pamphlet Series, no. 3, (ed. Johannes Riedel; St. Paul: Lutheran Society for Worship, Music and the Arts, 1958), 8–9.

[18] Ibid., 9.

the fact of his approaching marriage. Five days after the letters from Melanchthon and Luther were written, Walter, in June 1526, married Anna Hesse in Torgau. This union was blessed with one son, Johann (1727–78).[19]

John the Steadfast, however, refused to change his mind. Despite the protests of both Luther and Melanchthon, he suggested that musicians were too frequently a lazy group of people with not enough to do. In deference to Walter, however, the Elector granted him an annual allowance that he was to receive for the rest of his life because "this man Walter is not equipped to do other work."[20]

Following the disbanding of the *Hofkapelle*, Walter, in 1526, assumed the position of cantor at the Municipal Latin School in Torgau—a school attended at that time by more than 170 boys.[21] With his new work as cantor, Johann Walter thus becomes "the first cantor ever in the Lutheran church."[22] He also assumed the job as director of the *Stadtkantorei*, a group of the citizens of Torgau—musical amateurs—who met together to sing and study music under Walter's direction. This example of a voluntary choral organization interested in maintaining a high level of music in the church was soon followed elsewhere. From 1534 on, Walter was also responsible for teaching Latin and religion at the Torgau school. During his years at Torgau, Walter's choir included at various times Luther's son John,[23] the fathers of Leonhard Schroeter and Michael Praetorius, and Georg Otto, the teacher of Heinrich Schuetz.

It is difficult to overestimate the importance of the school and the *Schulkantorei* in the development of music during the Reformation period. Typical of many of the schools was the division into three groups: *elementarien, secunda*, and *summa*. The smaller boys received basic instruction in music because they would become choirboys upon entering the

---

[19] Walter's son, Johann, attended the Latin school in Torgau in the 1540s, and on November 30, 1551, he married Elizabeth Crodel, the daughter of Marcus Crodel, headmaster of the Torgau school. He subsequently became a music teacher. In 1553 he is known to have sung in the chapel choir of the Elector Moritz of Saxony, ultimately working as a granary steward. Four of his compositions survive.

[20] From the *Corpus Reformatorum,* vol. 1, no. 385 (1834): 799, and quoted in Wilibald Gurlitt, "Johannes Walter u. die Musik der Reformationszeit," *Lutherjahrbuch* XV (1933): 35.

[21] See Reese, op. cit., 677.

[22] Martin Brecht, *Martin Luther: Shaping and Defining the Reformation (1521–1532)* (trans. James L. Schaaf; Minneapolis: Fortress, 1994), 254.

[23] See *LW* 53:231–33. In 1542 Luther wrote to Marcus Crodel, headmaster of the Torgau school, to commend his son John to him and especially also for the study of music under Johann Walter.

next division. Boys from the second and third groups comprised the church choir and devoted considerable time to learning the hymns and the liturgy.[24] As Herbert Nuechterlein has pointed out: "A Lutheran service without the singing of the *Schulkantorei* or one of the music classes was practically inconceivable."[25] They helped cultivate an interest in music throughout the community and inspired congregations to more active participation in the service. School choirs were often the focal point of many communities, and the townspeople took pride in them. It was for groups such as these, particularly the school and civic singing groups at Torgau, that Walter devoted his greatest attention.

Walter, like many musicians of his day, was not only a composer but a poet as well. In 1538, while at Torgau, he published a rhymed homage to music, *Lob und Preis der loeblichen Kunst Musica* (*In Praise of the Noble Art of Music*),[26] a didactic poem of 324 lines, in which he developed an entire theology of music, following the ideas of Luther's scattered remarks on the subject. The occasion for this poem was apparently one of the Torgau town choir festivals.[27] In this poem Walter sees the origin of music not in metaphysics but in Christian salvation, that is, man's capabilities in music depend on the extent to which he lives in the grace of God. Setting forth the reasons why God had given the art of music to man, Walter wrote:

> *That such unmerited free grace*
> (Which God from love for all our race
> Had promised in His Word) *might be*
> *Kept fresh in human memory*
> *And move the heart to high delight*
> *In praising God both day and night—*
>
> *This is the weightiest reason why*
> *God music did at once supply.*

---

[24] For a fuller description of music in Luther's own education as a young child, see Carl Schalk, *Luther on Music: Paradigms of Praise* (St. Louis: Concordia, 1988).

[25] Herbert Nuechterlein, "The Sixteenth-Century Kantorei and Its Predecessors," *Church Music* 71.1 (1971): 3–8.

[26] This remarkable poem consists of 162 rhyming couplets. See Appendix B for a translation of this poem, together with a new translation of Luther's introduction to Walter's poem, both by F. Samuel Janzow. Another translation of Luther's introduction may be found in *LW* 53:319–20.

[27] See J. Stahlmann, foreword to Johann Walter, *Saemtliche Werke*, vol. 6 (eds. O. Schroeder and M. Schneider; Kassel u. Basel: Baerenreiter Verlag, 1953–73), xxvi–xxvii.

Then too, since sin acquired at birth
  Would bring to Adam's seed on earth
Much woe and—earth itself now spoiled—
  Small joy in all for which they toiled,
As antidote against that blight,
  To keep man's life from wilting quite,
And also to rejoice the heart,
  God soon supplied sweet music's art.
                    [Emphasis mine]

· ·

I have just named two reasons why
  God gave us music from on high.
These reasons teach us we must use
  The gift from heaven as God would choose:
By it let God be glorified;
  Then let it be our help and guide.[28]

Luther himself provided a rhymed introduction to this poem entitled "Vorrhede auff all gute Gesangbuecher" ("A Preface for All Good Hymnals").[29] Luther put his preface on the lips of *Frau Musica* (Lady Music) and had her extol her own gifts. Luther's introduction, together with Walter's more elaborately conceived poem, provide remarkable insights into the early Reformation's view of music.

As further evidence of the industry and diligence with which Walter pursued his work at Torgau are the so-called Torgau Walter-manuscripts.[30] These sources, in addition to the material published elsewhere, contain a number of anonymous pieces most likely from Walter's pen, such as hymns, Introits, Kyries, Magnificats, psalms, a Sequence, and short settings of the Preces together with various Responses. These Torgau Walter-manuscripts also included the eight Magnificats in Latin (1540),[31] the even-numbered verses set in simple homophonic style, probably intended for use in the daily Vespers; the two Passions in German according to

---

[28] See note 26.

[29] Luther's "A Preface for All Good Hymnals" was not printed in any hymnal in Luther's lifetime except in Joseph Klug's hymnal of 1543, where it was included at the end.

[30] These consist of a Nuremberg tenor part (ca. 1539), a Nuremberg bass part (before 1548), the Berlin *Chorbuch* (ca. 1540), the Weimar *Chorbuch* (ca. 1542), the Gotha *Chorbuch* (1545), and a set of partbooks from Berlin (1542–44).

[31] *SW* 4.

Fig. 2. The Castle Church at Torgau as it appears today. This was the first church built as a Lutheran church after the Reformation. Note the pulpit on the south wall.

Matthew and John;[32] modal settings of psalms in Latin based on the Gregorian psalm tones with the *cantus firmus* found either in the discantus or tenor parts; as well as a Magnificat[33] and the *Cantiones septum vocum.*[34]

The Passion settings are worthy of particular mention. The turba choruses are set in simple four-part homophonic style while the narrative is chanted to simple formulary melodies centering on f for Christ, c for the Evangelist, and f¹ for the other characters. "Walter played a decisive role in establishing this kind of narrative form in the German evangelical service,"[35] and in their radical simplicity, they clearly reflect his attitude that the words of the text receive primary attention and that they be set forth without musical interpretation by the composer. Walter also adopted the custom from the ancient plainsong Passions in which, after the death of Jesus, a pause is indicated for silent meditation by the worshipers. In Walter's *St. John Passion,* a pause is indicated to allow silent prayer (the Lord's Prayer), a practice allowing for the growing importance of greater participation and more thoughtful understanding on the part of the congregation.[36] Walter's Passions were widely used—in Leipzig as late as the early 1700s—and stand at the beginning of a development which culminated some two hundred years later in the settings of Johann Sebastian Bach (Ex. 6).

From this period also come the *Fugen auf die acht tonos zwei- und drei-Stimmig sonderlich auf Zinken* (1542), two- and three-part canons to be played "on any instruments of equal range, especially on cornetts" and particularly addressed "to young people, being especially easy to perform." Walter's only textless compositions, their intent was most probably didactic and instructional.

On October 3, 1544, the newly built Chapel of the Castle Hartenfels in Torgau—the first church building built by Lutherans—was dedicated. Luther was preacher for the service, and among the persons present were Melanchthon and Elector John the Magnanimous. For this unique occasion, Walter composed an homage-motet in five sections for seven voices based on Psalm 119.[37] Its uniqueness lies in that while the psalm text is set

---

[32] *SW* 4.

[33] All the preceding are found in *SW* 6.

[34] *SW* 5.

[35] From the foreword to *SW* 4.

[36] On this point, see Basil Smallman, *The Background of Passion Music: J. S. Bach and His Predecessors* (2d rev. and enlarged ed.; New York: Dover Publications, 1970), 24.

[37] This was the first of two psalm settings in the *Cantiones septum vocum.*

for four tenor voices in canon at the unison—the descant providing the counterpoint—a single repeated note in the alto part proclaims throughout the entire piece *"Vivat, vivat Ioannes Friderich, vivat Elector et Dux Saxonum; vivat defensor veri dogmatis . . ."* in honor of the Elector, while the bass part, a trumpet-like figure of five notes, presents the words *"Vivat Lutheri, vive Melanthon* [sic], *vive nostrae Lumina terrae, Charaque Christo Pecatora . . ."* throughout the work.[38]

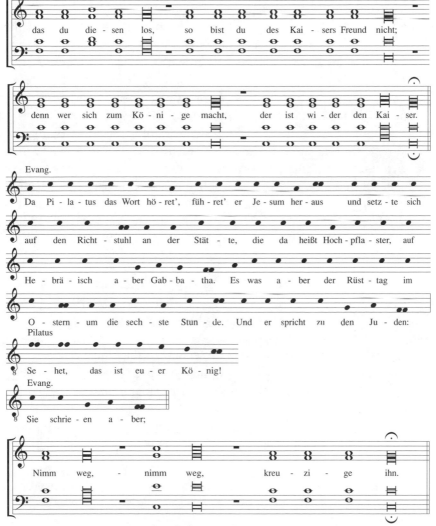

Ex. 6. Johann Walter, from *St. John Passion*

---

[38] It seems quite possible that a movement by Dufay based on the words *"Et in terra pax"* served as a model in this regard for Walter. See *Denkmaeler der Tonkunst in Oesterreich*, vol. 7, 145.

All these materials reflect Walter's systematic and well-ordered approach to providing music for the full round of Lutheran services. It is principally in connection with his work at Torgau that Walter earned the title of "first Lutheran cantor" and is affectionately called by many the "father of Lutheran church music."

Walter at Dresden (1548–54)

With the death of Luther in 1546 and a series of political events that shook Saxony and Germany, a period of trouble and trial began for Walter. Charles V, emperor of the Holy Roman Empire, made peace with the Turks and planned to deal with the Protestant rebels. A period of war between Catholics and Protestants ensued with Charles V winning a great victory over the Protestants in 1547. John the Steadfast, Elector of Saxony, was replaced by Moritz as the new Elector of Saxony.

Then in 1548, at the invitation of Moritz, the new Elector of Saxony, Walter moved to Dresden—the new residence of the Elector—to organize and direct the music for the court chapel, a position for which Melanchthon had recommended Walter. Walter spent six unhappy years at Dresden, serving a court which he felt had been religiously compromised by the Leipzig Interim agreement of 1548.[39] He was hesitant to change his strongly held religious, musical, or liturgical convictions, and in 1554, at the age of 58, Walter retired from his service at Dresden to return to his hometown of Torgau where his son still resided.

Walter Returns to Torgau (1554–70)

After his return to Torgau, Walter completed his *Magnificat octo tonorum* (1557),[40] a set of eight polyphonic Magnificats that demonstrates his mature skill. One opinion of these works suggests that "Walter prepared these settings with an unusual amount of love and that they represent the apex of his art."[41] Also belonging to this period is Walter's second large poem in praise of music, his *Lob und Preis der himmlischen Kunst Musica* (1564).[42]

Walter remained a staunch defender of Luther and Lutheranism until the end of his life. His last large-scale work—*Das christlich Kinderlied D.*

---

[39] During his time in Dresden, Walter kept his family and the choirboys who lived in his house away from the communion services conducted by the clergy who had submitted to the Leipzig Interim. See the foreword to *SW* 6, xix.

[40] *SW* 5.

[41] Quoted from Walter E. Buszin's English translation of the foreword to *SW* 5, viii.

[42] *SW* 6. This poem, consisting of 56 stanzas of six lines per stanza, is constructed as an acrostic, the first letter of each group of six lines spells out the word *Musica* in either ascending or descending order. Little else is known about the poem's origin.

Martini Lutheri Erhalt uns Herr (1566)[43]—was a collection of polyphonic music for four to six voices, at the center of which was Walter's setting of Luther's "very last hymn."[44] It was a final tribute to the reformer with whom Walter had been so close and for whose cause he had devoted his life's work. On March 25, 1570, Walter died in Torgau at the age of 74, and he was buried in the Church of the Holy Cross. No picture of Walter is known to exist.

Walter's name may be safely ascribed to the following hymn texts:

> "Allein auf Gottes Wort will ich"
> "Holdseliger, mein Herzens Trost"
> "Herzlich tut mich erfreuen" (a long poem of 33 stanzas)
> "Wach auf, wach auf, du deutsches Land" (a hymn of 26 stanzas
>   for which Walter wrote both text and music)

Excerpted stanzas from several of these poems appear in some hymnals as separate hymns (e.g., "The Bridegroom Soon Will Call Us" [*Lutheran Worship* 176, *The Lutheran Hymnal* 76]). In addition to these hymns, Walter also wrote a number of short verses, mottos, and humanistic glosses; two larger poems in praise of music already cited; two epitaphs on the death of Luther (1546) and John the Magnanimous (1556); three didactic and polemic poems in defense of Luther and refuting the doctrine of free will; and a table grace.[45]

Johann Walter's dedication to his work at Torgau established his name in the history of church music as the prototype of the Lutheran cantor and the first composer of the Lutheran church. While he was modest about his own ability as a composer, nevertheless Walter exerted considerable influence on those who followed him. His modest fame is reflected in the appearance of Walter manuscripts in many parts of northern and southern Germany, Hungary, and Denmark.

Although Walter may not be counted among the first-rank composers of history, he was a master of the contrapuntal technique of his day, particularly the use of canonic devices. He was among the first to use in his music Luther's translation of the Bible in the vernacular. Walter's approach was thoroughly liturgical, and he composed church music in

---

[43] *SW* 6.

[44] Luther's very last hymn was most probably the German version of "O lux beata trinitas," which is missing from Walter's collection of 1524 and which probably had not come to Walter's attention. It was included in the Klug collection of 1543. However, in Walter's memory, "Erhalt uns Herr" had become Luther's last will and testament.

[45] All these are found in *SW* 6.

which the chorale was at the center of the great majority of his works.

Walter's models were such composers as Josquin, Heinrich Isaac, Adam of Fulda, Ludwig Senfl, Conrad Rupsch, and Adam Rener. His work was clearly related to the theology of the church and his understanding—which he derived from Luther—that the role of music in the church was to *proclaim* the Word rather than to *interpret* it. This is clearly seen in Walter's adherence to the older *cantus-firmus* technique in which the unchanging melody in the tenor is the basic element in his musical structures, the other voices weaving a polyphonic texture—often of some complexity—about the tenor part. His technique in this regard is more closely related to that of the earlier Renaissance than to his own immediate time.

In Walter's work one can see early intimations of the two directions in which Lutheran church music would proceed in the coming decades. These two directions were the development of the polyphonic motet style and, simultaneously, the development of the simpler homophonic cantional style. In setting Lutheran church music on these two paths, both of them closely tied to the chorale, Walter provided a bearing that would continue to guide the work of those Lutheran composers who were to follow him.

JOHANN WALTER

1490	1500	1510	1520	1530	1540	1550	1560	1570

Geystliche gesangk Buchleyn (1524)

Deutsche Passionen [Matthew & John] (1525–30)

Magnificat octo tonorum [simple] (1540)
Psalmen [homophonic style] (1540)

Fugen auf die acht tonos (1542)

Cantiones septum vocum (1544/45)

Magnificat octo tonorum [polyphonic] (1557)

Das christlich Kinderlied (1566)

Guide to Johann Walter's Collected Works

Walter, Johann. *Saemtliche Werke* (*SW*). Edited by O. Schroeder and M.
    Schneider. 6 vols. Kassel u. Basel: Baerenreiter Verlag, and St.
    Louis: Concordia, 1953–73.

The following works are listed in chronological order.

1524   *Geystliche gesangk Buchleyn* (*SW* 1, 2, 3)
            The first edition contains 43 settings—38 in German, five
      in Latin—for four, five, and six voices. The *cantus firmus* in
      tenor part (except for four pieces) consisted of German
      chorales and Gregorian melodies. Later editions expanded the
      number of pieces, particularly those in Latin.
            SW 1 contains the German songs; *SW* 2 contains the Latin
      songs; and *SW* 3 contains those songs found in the earlier edi-
      tions but omitted in the final edition, as well as single com-
      positions that appear in various manuscripts and collections.
            More recent scholarship suggests the following history of
      publication: The first edition of 1524 was reprinted in 1525;
      a second edition (no longer extant) followed in 1528 with
      reprints in 1534 and 1537; a third edition appeared in 1544;
      and the final and fourth edition appeared in 1551.

1525–30   *Deutsche Passionen nach Matthaeus & Johannes* (*SW* 4)
            These Passions consist of turba choruses in simple homo-
      phonic style with chanted narrative.

1540   *Magnificat octo tonorum* (*SW* 4)
            Eight settings for four voices (one for five voices) of the
      even-numbered verses of the canticle in simple homophonic
      fauxbourdon style.

              Psalmen (*SW* 4)
            Eight Latin psalms (119, 128, 134, 110, 138, 143, 122, 144)
      in simple homophonic *fauxbourdon* style.

1542   *Fugen auf die acht tonos zwei- und drei-Stimmig sonderlich
      auf Zinken* (*SW* 4)
            Twenty-six two- and three-part canons for equal instru-
      ments.

1544/45   *Cantiones septum vocum* (*SW* 5)
            Two seven-voice psalms (119 and 120), the first of which
            was written for the dedication of the chapel at Castle
            Hartenfels.

1557   *Magnificat octo tonorum* (*SW* 5)
            Four-, five-, and six-voice polyphonic settings of the even-
            numbered verses in Latin. Settings in the fifth, seventh, and
            eighth modes have complete settings of the Gloria Patri.

1566   *Das christlich Kinderlied D. Martini Lutheri Erhalt uns
            Herr* (*SW* 6)
            Twenty-one polyphonic pieces in German and Latin; 19
            anonymous pieces in Latin from the Torgau-Walter manu-
            scripts; poems without music.

Selected References for Further Reading

Primary Source:
Walter, Johann. *Saemtliche Werke.* Edited by O. Schroeder and M.
    Schneider. 6 vols. Kassel u. Basel: Baerenreiter Verlag, and St.
    Louis: Concordia, 1953–73.
            The English translation of several of the forewords are
            especially helpful: foreword to *SW* 1 (in *SW* 3) translated by
            Walter E. Buszin; foreword to *SW* 3 translated by Walter E.
            Buszin; foreword to *SW* 4 translated by Margaret Bent; fore-
            word to *SW* 5 translated by Walter E. Buszin; and foreword to
            SW 6 translated by John A. Parkinson.

Secondary Sources:
Blankenburg, Walter. "Walter, Johann." Cols. 192–201 in vol. 14 of *Die
    Musik in Geschichte und Gegenwart.* Kassel u. Basel: Baerenreiter,
    1968.
————. *Johann Walter Leben und Werke.* Edited by Friedhelm
    Brusniak. Tutzing: Hans Schneider, 1991.
Blume, Friedrich. *Renaissance and Baroque Music: A Comprehensive
    Survey.* Translated by M. D. Herter Norton. New York: W. W.
    Norton & Co., 1967. Originally published in *Die Musik in
    Geschichte und Gegenwart.*

Braun, Werner. "Walter, Johann." Pages 188–89 in vol. 20 of *The New Grove Dictionary of Music and Musicians*. Edited by Stanley Sadie. New York: Macmillan, 1980.

Buszin, Walter E. "Johann Walter: Composer, Pioneer, and Luther's Musical Consultant." Pages 78–110 in vol. 3 of *The Musical Heritage of the Church*. Edited by Theodore Hoelty-Nickel. Valparaiso: Valparaiso University Press, 1946.

Ehmann, Wilhelm. "Johann Walter. Der erste Kantor der prot. Kirche." *Musik und Kirche* VI (1934): 188–203, 240–46.

Gurlitt, Wilibald. "Johannes Walter u. die Musik der Reformationszeit." *Lutherjahrbuch* XV (1933): 1–112.

Leaver, Robin. "The Lutheran Reformation." Pages 263–85 in *The Renaissance: From the 1470s to the End of the 16th Century*. Edited by Iain Fenlon. Englewood Cliffs: Prentice Hall, 1989.

———. "Johann Walter's Reputation and the Publication of His Music in England and America." Pages 145–69 in *Johann Walter Studien: Tagungsbericht Torgau 1996*. Edited by Friedhelm Brusniak. Tutzing: Hans Schneider, 1998.

Reese, Gustav. "The Earliest Music of the Lutherans: The Role of Luther; Walter." Pages 673–78 in *Music in the Renaissance*. Rev. ed. New York: W. W. Norton & Co., 1959.

3

Georg Rhau

Printer of Early Reformation Music

That the beginning of the Reformation should coincide so closely with the development and spread of printing was to be of crucial significance. The refinement of the printing process which ensued from Gutenberg's work made possible the relatively inexpensive production of a wide range of booklets, broadsheets, and pamphlets which would help spread the Reformation throughout Europe. It should not be surprising that the church of the Word and the church of the book should look with favor on and use to the utmost the technological revolution begun by Gutenberg in the middle of the 15th century.

By 1500 there were enterprising printers and printing establishments in some 60 German cities. By the time the Reformation was gaining momentum, many of them were providing the "new song" of the church on broadsheets and in a variety of smaller and larger collections of hymns. Among these printers were Jobst Gutknecht in Nuremberg; Rauscher in Erfurt; Valentin Babst in Leipzig; Michael Lotther of Magdeburg; Johannes Loersfeld and Mathes Maler in Erfurt; Peter Schoeffer probably of Worms; Joseph Klug, Hans Luft, and Hans Weiss in Wittenberg; and others in Augsburg and Ulm. Printers in Breslau and Zwickau would make their contribution, as would Schoeffer and Apiarius and Wolf Koepphel in Strassburg. As a city at the heart of the Reformation, Wittenberg would assume a particularly important role in the publication of music for the Reformation church. At the center of music publishing activity in Wittenberg would be the person of Georg Rhau.

Georg Rhau (Rhaw), an older contemporary of Johann Walter by eight years, was born in 1488, just five years after Luther, in Franconia in the town of Eisfeld on the Werra River. While little is known of his early life, in 1508 Rhau was in attendance at the University of Erfurt, and from 1512 he attended the University at Wittenberg, where he received his bachelor of arts degree in 1514. For the next four years, Rhau worked in the Wittenberg printing establishment of Rhau-Grunenberg, presumably owned by his uncle. It was an apprenticeship in which Rhau undoubtedly gained valuable experience that would stand him in good stead when he opened his own publishing house upon his return to Wittenberg in

Fig. 3. Georg Rhau

1523.[1] In 1518 Rhau became cantor at the *Thomasschule* and the *Thomaskirche* in Leipzig, thus becoming a predecessor of Johann Sebastian Bach. Rhau held the position at least until 1520. Upon his arrival in Leipzig, he also became associated with the faculty at the University of Leipzig, where he lectured on music theory.

About the time of his arrival in Leipzig, Rhau published his *Enchiridion utriusque musicae practicae*,[2] a treatise on music theory devoted to the subject of plainchant (*musica choralis*). It was followed a few years later by the *Enchiridion musicae mensuralis* (Leipzig, 1520), which dealt with the subject of polyphony (*musica figuralis*). Both treatises, often bound together as one volume, were intended for music students, and they achieved remarkable success, being republished in successive editions past the middle of the century, the last edition being published in 1553.[3]

It was during the period when Rhau was cantor at the *Thomaskirche* in Leipzig that the famous Leipzig debate occurred—a disputation between Johann Eck and the Wittenberg Reformers, Andreas Carlstadt and Martin Luther, which lasted from June 27 to July 14, 1519. The debate was held in the great hall of the castle Pleissenburg in Leipzig. It was to be a turning point in the development of the Reformation. For this occasion, Rhau wrote a 12-voiced *Missa de Sancto Spiritu* and a Te Deum which, unfortunately, are not preserved. Schwiebert describes the scene at the Leipzig debate in the following way.

> The Leipzig debate opened with much pomp and ceremony on June 27, 1519. Simon Pistoris, a professor from the department of Jurisprudence, delivered the address of welcome in the large auditorium of the principal college building located on Ritterstrasse. The group then attended Mass in the Thomaskirche, for which occasion Cantor Georg Rhau had prepared special

---

[1] The Rhau-Grunenberg printing establishment was particularly important in the early period of the Reformation because it printed Luther's first publication, as well as a number of other early Reformation documents. See Martin Brecht, *Martin Luther: His Road to Reformation 1483–1521* (trans. James L. Schaaf; Minneapolis: Fortress, 1993), 119, 143, 218, 282, 290.

[2] Georg Rhau, *Enchiridion utriusque musicae practicae* (Facsimile edition, ed. Hans Albrecht; Kassel u. Basel: Baerenreiter, 1951).

[3] See Carl Parrish, "A Renaissance Music Manual for Choirboys," in *Aspects of Medieval and Renaissance Music: A Birthday Offering to Gustave Reese* (ed. Jan LaRue; New York: W. W. Norton & Co., 1966), 649–64.

choir music for twelve voices. . . . To close the preliminary service, the St. Thomas Choir sang and the town band played the familiar hymn "Veni, sancte Spiritus", while the whole audience knelt.[4]

One result of the debate was that many were won over to Luther's view. This event was apparently Rhau's first significant encounter with the Reformation. One year after the disputation Rhau was forced to resign his Leipzig position on the basis of his newly adopted adherence to the Reformer's teachings.

From 1520 to 1522, Rhau served as a schoolmaster in Eisleben and Hildburghausen, eventually returning to Wittenberg in 1523, where he set up a business as printer and publisher. In this capacity, he issued many first editions of Luther's writings—among them the first edition of the Large Catechism and the Augsburg Confession—and, most important, many collections of musical works which helped to shape the direction of early Lutheran church music. From 1541 on, Rhau served as a member of the Wittenberg town council. In 1548, the year of his death, Rhau became director of the electoral choir at Torgau, briefly succeeding Johann Walter, who had been invited by Moritz, the new Elector of Saxony, to take a position in Dresden to organize and direct the music for the court chapel. On August 6, 1548, Rhau died in Wittenberg, where he was buried with full academic honors. All university classes were dismissed so the student body and faculty could participate in the funeral service.

Rhau enjoyed a close friendship with both Luther and Melanchthon and gained fame as the *typographus Wittenbergensi*, the official printer of Wittenberg and, in large part, the Reformation. He must also be ranked as the most gifted printer and publisher of the Lutheran church in the 16th century. His uniqueness for the purposes of this discussion is to be found in the many and varied musical publications which he produced which helped to point Lutheran church music in the direction it was to pursue for the remainder of the 16th century.

Perhaps the greatest accomplishment of Rhau was in laying out a large-scale plan for providing the Lutheran church with the music needed for its worship and then, as printer and publisher, pursuing the realization of that plan in actual collections and music publications. Leo Schrade suggests that Rhau's importance is to be found in "his genius as an organizer, one who through his profound ideas made his publications serve the purposes of the renewal of Christian doctrine, and who, moreover, made music a reality in the services of the Church."[5]

---

[4] See E. G. Schwiebert, *Luther and His Times* (St. Louis: Concordia, 1950), 393, 413. See also Gustav Reese, *Music in the Renaissance* (rev. ed.; New York: W. W. Norton & Co., 1959), 678.

[5] Leo Schrade, "The Editorial Practice of Georg Rhaw," in vol. 4 of *The Musical Heritage of the Church* (ed. Theodore Hoelty-Nickel; St. Louis: Concordia, 1954), 31.

Rhau published many important musical collections and treatises[6]—among the early publications was a textbook of music fundamentals by Martin Agricola entitled *Ein kurtz deudsche Musica* (1528), a publication so successful that subsequent editions were published by Rhau in 1529 and 1533. Of particular interest was Rhau's publication of Agricola's *Musica instrumentalis deudsch* (1529, revised and expanded in 1545), which promoted the cause of instrumental music on both theological and practical bases, and Agricola's *Musica figuralis deudsch* (1532).[7] In the *Musica instrumentalis deudsch,* Agricola argues the case for instrumental music. Those who object for one reason or another

> . . . also say "Art must be held back, so that art will endure." When one expresses oneself in this manner, it may well give an illusion and a good appearance to the world, but to God it is truly unchristian, indeed quite heathen talk; and I look forward to seeing how they will fare at the Last Judgment, when God will say to them, "I have graced you with great art, with particular understanding, and I have heaped riches on you, so that through them you would serve your neighbor and communicate these things. But you have kept them for yourselves and have used them for your own pleasure, fame and pride." Then they will surely see what kind of excuse and apology it is to say, "Art must be held back, so that art will endure."[8]

In the revised edition of 1545, Agricola speaks of the art of instrumental music as a medium to ". . . praise God, who has given this delightful and joyous art . . . to us dejected and miserable men in this vale of tears, so that we might praise Him in many musical ways, namely with singing and playing of wind and stringed instruments like the royal prophet David and also Moses, Solomon, etc."[9] Against those who scorn instrumental music, Agricola simply suggests that

> . . . you will not follow them, but rather Moses, David and many other excellent people who have thought very highly of [instrumental music] (as the Psalter etc. indicates) and have presented and bequeathed us examples of

---

[6] A listing of music publications issued from Rhau's printing establishment from 1528 to 1548 may be found in Victor H. Mattfeld, *Georg Rhaw's Publications for Vespers,* Musicological Studies XI (Brooklyn: Institute of Mediaeval Music, 1966), 351–53.

[7] For additional information regarding Agricola and Rhau, see the preface to *The Musica instrumentalis deudsch of Martin Agricola: A treatise on musical instruments, 1529 and 1545* (trans. and ed. William E. Hettrick; Cambridge: Cambridge University Press, 1994).

[8] From the dedication to the *Musica instrumentalis deudsch.* op. cit., 4.

[9] From the preface to the 1545 edition of *Musica instrumentalis deudsch,* op. cit., 63–64.

how to praise God in various ways. Now in our own time, among many others, Dr. Martin Luther . . . also does the same thing.[10]

Rhau's publication of Agricola's work was a strong endorsement of the use of instruments not only in the education of young men, but also the use of instruments in the worship of the church.

In the years before 1538, Rhau largely limited himself to the publication of music primers for the cantors of the Reformation, his own textbooks, and material by such persons as Martin Agricola, Nikolaus Listenius, Johann Spangenberg, Johann Gallicus, and Johann Walter. After 1538, Rhau began work on the organization of his large-scale practical editions together with a variety of music, both sacred and secular, for daily use by the choirs of the Municipal Latin schools.

Rhau's greatest achievement, however, is to be found in the series of collections that he published from 1538 to 1545 in Wittenberg, which began to provide in a systematic way for the needs of the various Lutheran services. Whatever the reasons might be for the hiatus between the initiation of his printing business and the beginning of this series of 15 collections of music, these important publications exerted an influence that is difficult to overestimate. In every one of the collections, it is clear that liturgical considerations were uppermost in Rhau's mind.

Of particular interest are the prefaces to the various collections, many of which were written by Luther, Melanchthon, and Bugenhagen, in addition to Rhau himself. They clearly set out the musical, liturgical, and theological bases on which music in Lutheran worship was to proceed: music is of divine origin and is God's gift to man; the end of music is the glorification of God; and music, from a Lutheran viewpoint, is to serve in the proclamation and propagation of the Word. Thus the purpose of music is to sound forth the Gospel in the world. Melanchthon went so far as to say that where singing and religious music ceases, it is to be feared that the holy doctrine itself will die.[11] All these prefaces attest to the Reformation conviction that the singer or musician is in fact a preacher of the Gospel. For these collections, Rhau drew on a wide variety of composers, both old and new, both Catholic and Lutheran.

The 15 collections published by Rhau between 1538 and 1545 group themselves into three larger categories: publications for the Mass; publications for Vespers; and publications for a variety of other purposes. The collections were printed as sets of partbooks. A summary of the contents of these collections follows.

---

[10] Ibid., 65.

[11] Schrade, op. cit., 31.

Publications for the Mass
The collections designed for use in the Mass were four in number.

1538   *Selectae harmoniae . . . de passione domini*
            The preface is by Philipp Melanchthon. This collection
            included two motet-like Passions by Galliculus and Longaval
            (frequently ascribed to Obrecht), Lamentations, an *Oratio
            Jeremiae,* a Passion motet cycle, and single Passion motets.
            Protestant and Catholic composers are about equally bal-
            anced and represented by such contributors as Longaval,
            Isaac, Compere, Senfl, Walter, Galliculus, Ducis, Lemlin,
            Cellarius, Eckel, and Stahel. The organization is relatively
            loose compared with some of the later publications.

1539   *Officia paschalia de resurrectione et ascensione Domini*
            Contains a through-composed Easter Mass by Johannes
            Galliculus; an incomplete Easter Mass by Johannes
            Alectorius; a third Mass put together from works of Konrad
            Rein and Adam Rener, with other sections by Thomas
            Stoltzer; Easter motets; an Easter psalm by Senfl and others;
            and Masses for Ascension.
            As an example, the Easter Mass by Galliculus consisted of
            Introit with verse, Kyrie, Gloria, Alleluia with verse, the
            three-part Easter Sequence *Agnus redemit oves,* Gospel with
            salutation, Sanctus with Pleni and Benedictus, Agnus Dei,
            and Communion. The dedication of the work is by Rhau.

1541   *Opus decem missarum . . .*
            Ten four-part Masses for Sunday and ferial use "to the ben-
            efit of the schools and all students of music" by such com-
            posers as Johannes Stahel, Adam Rener, Heinrich Isaac,
            Petrus Roselli, Pipelare, Sampson, and Senfl.
            The compositions are generally quite conservative. The
            majority of the Masses are based on secular melodies.

1545   *Officiorum (ut vocant) de nativitate, circumcisione, epipha-
            nia Domini . . .*
            The preface is by Melanchthon. Similar in content and
            arrangement to the *Officia paschalia* (1539).

From the *Officia paschalia* (1539), the following excerpt from the
"Kyrie paschali" would be typical (Ex. 7). This ninefold Kyrie alternates
chant with polyphonic settings in the following way:

Kyrie	Chant
Kyrie	Polyphony
Kyrie	Chant
Christe	Polyphony
Christe	Chant
Christe	Polyphony
Kyrie	Chant
Kyric	Polyphony
Kyrie	Chant

The polyphony carries the chant melody in the tenor part in accordance with conventional practice of the time, thus integrating each of the sections and giving a rich and unified coherence to the whole.

Ex. 7. Georg Rhau, "Kyrie paschali" from the *Officia paschalia*

Publications for Vespers

Rhau prepared six collections for use in connection with Vespers. These collections included: a) three volumes which were compilations of the works of various composers, and b) three volumes which were the work of single composers—Sixtus Dietrich and Balthasar Resinarius. The Vespers group of publications was the most strictly organized and encompassed all the pieces that the pupils had to sing in the daily Vespers. The material was organized either according to the days of the week (*Vesperarum precum officia* and Dietrich's antiphons) or the *de tempore* of the year (both hymn collections and Resinarius' responsories).

1540   *Vesperarum precum officia psalmi feriarium et dominicalium dierum totius anni . . .*
            The preface is by Georg Rhau. These works for four voices are arranged in the form of complete services. For each weekday Vesper service there is provided: antiphon with five psalms in four-part chordal settings based on the psalm tones, a responsory with verse, one or more hymns, versicle, Magnificat with proper antiphon—all in simple chordal settings. Johann Walter's Magnificat cycle in all the modes in simple *fauxbourdon* settings is included.
            Composers include Walter (21 compositions), Stoltzer, Isaac, Rener, Ducis, Georg Forster (nine), Galliculus, Stahel (37), Cellarius, and Andreas Cappelus.

1541   *Novum ac insigne opus musicum triginta sex antiphonarum*
            One of the single-composer volumes, this work contains 36 antiphons by Sixtus Dietrich.

1542   *Sacrorum hymnorum liber primus*
            Preface by Georg Rhau. A collection of 134 hymns by Stoltzer, Finck, von Bruck, Isaac, Josquin, Rener, Walter, Senfl, Resinarius (under the name of Harzer), Breitengraser, Stoltzer, Poepel, Gresinger, Obrecht, Cellarius, Haugk, Eckel, Cappelus, and others. (This collection appears in *Das Erbe deutsche Musik,* 1 Reihe, vols. 21 and 25 edited by R. Gerber, Leipzig, 1942/43.)

1543   *Responsorum numero octoginta de tempore . . . ; liber*
        secundus responsorum de sanctis . . .
        One of the single-composer volumes. Preface by Bugen-
        hagen. This volume contains 80 responsories by Balthasar
        Resinarius.

1544   *Postremum vespertini officii opus . . .*
        Includes 25 polyphonic settings of the Latin Magnificat,
        one psalm, and one "Domine, libera me," both also in Latin.
        The Magnificats appear without antiphons and are either
        through-composed settings of all the verses or, in the majori-
        ty of cases, polyphonic settings only of the even-numbered
        verses. The organization is chiefly by mode without de tem-
        pore or de sancte considerations.
        Composers included in this collection are Galliculus,
        Rener, La Rue, Divitis, Pipelare, Iachet, Fevin, Richafort,
        Verdelot, Morales, Tugdual, and Pieton.

1545   *Novum opus musicum tres tomos sacrorum hymnorum*
        continens
        One of the single-composer volumes, this work contains
        122 settings by Sixtus Dietrich. In a sense it can be consid-
        ered a second volume to that of 1541.

The *Vesperarum precum officia* (1540) provided, among other elements, antiphons for the psalms which were sung each weekday in the
Vesper services. The antiphons in four parts were written in a modest
polyphonic style with the psalmody sung in simple four-part chordal fashion in settings such as Johann Walter's. The antiphon shown in Ex. 8 is by
Johann Stahel. While Rhau knew well the value of great artistic motets, in
this collection he offered the simplest music to introduce young people to
polyphonic singing. Thus this antiphon by Johann Stahel—who was
responsible for almost a third of the settings here—is simple, short, and
modest in its musical demands.

The other large collection of music and Rhau's last work for the Vesper
services, the *Postremum vespertini officii opus* (1544), presented a collection of 25 Magnificats in which the entire text was set either polyphonically or—in the majority of cases—in which only the even-numbered
verses were set polyphonically, the odd-numbered verses being sung by
cantor or choir to the appropriate Gregorian tone. The following excerpt
(Ex. 9) from the third Magnificat by Iachet, which sets only the alternate
verses in polyphony, is typical.

Ex. 8. Johann Stahel, antiphon from the *Vesperarum precum officia* (1540)

Ex. 9. Iachet, alternate verse "Et exultavit" from the third Magnificat in *Postremum vespertini officii opus* (1544)

The four-part motet on the hymn "Veni Creator Spiritus" for the feast of Pentecost by Sixtus Dietrich (Ex. 10), taken from his *Novum opus musicum* (1545), is a straightforward example of a tenor *cantus-firmus* motet. The tenor part carries the chant melody in a slightly inflected form, the other voices using the general contour of the melody as they weave their polyphony around the central melody.

Ex. 10. Sixtus Dietrich, "Veni Creator Spiritus" from *Novum opus musicum* (1545)

Publications for a Variety of Purposes

A third set of Rhau's publications offered a variety of materials for various liturgical, pedagogical, and domestic purposes. There are five of these publications.

1538   *Symphoniae iucundae atque adeo breves . . .*

Preface by Martin Luther. This collection contains 52 Latin motets—including a few secular ones—ascribed to 24 Catholic composers, seven Protestant composers, and 21 anonymous composers.

Among the Catholic composers are Josquin, Brumel, La Rue, Mouton, Lapicida, Verdelot, de Sermissy, Richafort, Hellinck, and Lupi. Protestant composers are represented by such men as Walter, Forster, Ducis, and Eckel.

1542/45   *Tricinia . . . latina, germanica, brabantia, gallica* and *Bicinia gallica, latina, germanica . . . Tomus I; secundus tomus Biciniorum . . . gallica, latina, germanica*

The *Tricinia* contained 90 works in Latin, German, low German, and French. The two volumes of *Bicinia* contains French, German, and Latin works.

1544   *Newe deudsche geistliche Gesenge . . . fuer die gemeinen Schulen*

This work contains 123 compositions for three, four, five, and six voices by 19 composers (excluding 12 anonymous works which have optimistically been ascribed by some to Rhau), including Resinarius (30), von Bruck (17), Senfl (11), Ducis (10), Dietrich (eight), Hellinck (11), Mahu, Agricola, Forster, Heintz, Hauck, Pilitz, Braetel, Stahel, Stoltzer, Vogelhuber, Weinmann, and Walter.

This volume is a collection of pieces designed for the needs of the school choir and for worship. Its historical importance lies in the fact that it is the principal collection that reflects the state of German polyphonic song of this period.

1544/51   Reprints of Johann Walter's *Wittembergisch deudsch Geistlich Gesangbuechlein*

These are the third and fourth (final) editions of Walter's work, the last edition printed after Walter's death.

Of the first two publications of Rhau in 1538—the *Selectae harmoniae*, one of the collections for the Mass, and the *Symphoniae iucundae*—it was the *Symphoniae iucundae,* a collection of 52 motets for the Sundays of the church year, that has attracted the most attention. While Philipp Melanchthon had written the foreword for the former, it was Martin Luther's foreword to the latter which is often quoted and is regarded as one of the most important statements by Luther regarding art music. Some of the most quoted portions from this preface are as follows:

> I would certainly like to praise music with all my heart as the excellent gift of God which it is and to commend it to everyone. But I am so overwhelmed by the diversity and magnitude of its virtues and benefits that I can find neither beginning nor end or method for my discourse.
>
> We can mention only one point (which experience confirms), namely, that next to the Word of God, music deserves the highest praise. . . . For whether you wish to comfort the sad, to terrify the happy, to encourage the despairing, to humble the proud, to calm the passionate, or to appease those full of hate . . . what more effective means than music could you find? The Holy Ghost Himself honors her as an instrument for His proper work . . .
>
> . . . the gift of language combined with the gift of song was only given to man to let him know that he should praise God with both words and music, namely, by proclaiming [the Word of God] through music and by providing sweet melodies with words.
>
> But when [musical] learning is added to all this and artistic music which corrects, develops, and refines the natural music, then at last it is possible to taste with wonder (yet not to comprehend) God's absolute and perfect wisdom in his wondrous work of music.[12]

The collection was most likely intended not for professional choirs and cantors as much as for amateur singers and music lovers in general. The distinguishing mark of this collection is that Rhau selected material, largely from the old masters, which was relatively simple in rhythm and in its contrapuntal art. A good example would be the very first piece in the collection, Josquin's "In te, Domine, speravi" (Ex. 11). Rhau may have chosen to begin the collection with a selection from Josquin because the composer was a favorite of Luther or simply because such a piece was better suited to a more informal and unrehearsed situation than a more complicated motet.

---

[12] *LW* 53:321–24.

Ex. 11. Josquin, "In te, Domine, speravi" from the *Symphoniae iucundae* (1538)

In 1544 Rhau published one of his most important compilations—the *Newe deudsche geistliche Gesenge . . . fuer die gemeinen Schulen,* a collection of 123 compositions for three, four, five, and six voices by some of the leading composers of the day: Thomas Stoltzer, Ludwig Senfl, Balthasar Resinarius, Benedictus Ducis, Arnold von Bruck, Lupus Hellinck, and Sixtus Dietrich, among others. Among the compositions are 12 anonymous pieces, the majority of which some scholars have been ready to ascribe to Rhau himself. The collection was to serve as a resource for the Lutheran Latin schools of the day to "develop in young people an understanding of church music and ability to perform it, and thus to give church music an increasingly artistic character."[13] The importance of this collection is that it demonstrates the variety of ways the Reformation

    [13] Theodore Gerold, "Protestant Music on the Continent," in *The Age of Humanism: 1540–1630* (ed. Gerald Abraham; vol. 4 of *The New Oxford History of Music;* London: Oxford University Press, 1968), 430.

hymn was treated by the composers of the second quarter of the 16th century, as well as providing an insight into the repertoire that was used in the Latin schools of the time. The setting of "Veni, Creator Spiritus" by Balthasar Resinarius (Ex. 12) is a particularly fine example of the older tenor *cantus-firmus* style, the melody being carried by the tenor part in a simple, straightforward manner. It is interesting to compare this setting with that of Sixtus Dietrich cited earlier. The five-part setting by Georg Forster (Ex. 13) combines two melodies both originally used for Martin Luther's hymn "Vom Himmel hoch da komm ich her." The soprano *cantus firmus* ("Vom Himmel kam der Engel Schar") flows in counterpoint to the longer note tenor *cantus firmus* ("Vom Himmel hoch da komm ich her") while the other voices provide a marvelous counterpoint to both melodies.

Ex. 12. Balthasar Resinarius, "Veni, Creator Spiritus" from *Newe deudsche geistliche Gesenge* (1544)

Ex. 13. Georg Forster, "Vom Himmel hoch" from the *Newe deudsche geistliche Gesenge* (1544)

The final collection which Rhau prepared for use in the Lutheran Latin schools was the *Bicinia gallica, latina, germanica,* which appeared in 1545 in two volumes. It included texts, both sacred and secular, in a variety of languages. The purpose of these two-part pieces was pedagogical, enabling the boys to acquire the ability to sing two parts simultaneously. This skill would lead them to be able to sing three and four parts as they achieved greater facility, a fact attested to by the inclusion at the end of the *Secundus Tomus* of a number of pieces in three and four parts. The example given here, "Ein feste Burg ist unser Gott," is typical (Ex. 14).

Ex. 14. Johann Walter, "Ein feste Burg ist unser Gott" from the *Bicinia*

A listing of Rhau's publications is of importance—beyond the music itself—for what it reveals of the man and the way he saw his role in the emerging picture of music in the life of the Lutheran church. It is eminently clear that Rhau saw his own role not chiefly as a business, but rather as a "generative force for the production and dissemination of much-needed liturgical and extra-liturgical musical materials for the emerging curricular and worship demands of the protestant schools of the time, for the effective musical conduct of the divine services in the churches and schools, and for the cultural and recreational needs of the home and of society."[14] With such a large-scale vision of the task at hand, Rhau set out in a systematic way to provide the necessary materials. His publications are, in effect, an outline of that plan.

The prefaces to the various Rhau collections reflect his concern that music in Lutheran worship be set on a proper theological foundation. By involving such leaders of the Reformation as Melanchthon, Bugenhagen,

---

[14] Foreword to *Postremum verspertini officii opus,* ed. Paul G. Bunjes, vii.

and Luther himself as authors of some of these prefaces, Rhau's publications reflect a consensus about the role of music in worship quite unequaled elsewhere. The importance of the schools in the musical culture of the Lutheran church can be seen in the obviously pedagogical nature of some of these materials, as well as in the titles and dedications which frequently reflect their intended use in daily and weekly worship.

The ecumenical nature of these collections reflects the freedom which the early reformers and church musicians felt to choose from the useful compositions of Lutheran and Catholic composers alike. The contents of many of the volumes suggest that they would be equally useful in Catholic or Lutheran circumstances. Finally, the continuing emphasis on Latin in many of these collections demonstrates that Luther's concern for the use of the vernacular language in no way eliminated Latin from use in worship.

Rhau's collections reflect the compositional procedures that had been associated with liturgical texts in the period at the beginning and just prior to the Reformation—the generation of Obrecht and Ockeghem. But they also include the works of a younger generation of composers who were associated directly with the new church, many of whom are known largely through Rhau's publications. Thus the importance of these collections is also to be found in "the preservation of a repertory useful for the study of the early Reformation worship service, its music, and the conservative attitudes toward musical style held by its composers."[15] The collection is without equal in its time.

In the final analysis, Rhau's contribution to the music of the Lutheran church is based on his understanding and appreciation of the liturgy in which the music he published was to find its home and to his devotion to providing materials related to the chorale melodies of the Reformation. His training as composer, educator, and friend of numerous composers and reformers provided him with both the skills and opportunity to accomplish his goals. His publications reflect the standard choral repertoire of 16th-century Lutheranism as no others do.

---

[15] Victor H. Mattfeld, "Rhau, Georg," in vol. 15 of *The New Grove Dictionary of Music and Musicians* (ed. Stanley Sadie; New York: Macmillan, 1980), 788.

RHAU'S PUBLICATIONS from 1538 to 1545

1538   1540   1542   1544   1546

Symphoniae iucundae (1538)
Selectae harmoniae (1538)

Officia paschalia (1539)

Vesperarum precum officia (1540)

Opus decem missarum (1541)
Novum ac insigne opus musicum triginta sex antiphonarum (1541)

Sacrorum hymnorum liber primus (1542)
Tricinia (1542)

Responsorum numero octoginta de tempore (1543)

Postremum vespertini officii opus (1544)
Newe deudsche geistliche Gesenge (1544)
Reprints of Walter's Wittembergisch deudsch geistliche Gesangbuechlein (1544/51)

Officiorum (ut vocant) (1545)
Novum opus musicum (1545)
Bicinia (1545)

Guide to Georg Rhau's Publications

Rhau, Georg. *Musikdrucke aus den Jahren 1538 bis 1545 in praktischer Neuausgabe (Mu)*. General editor Hans Albrecht. Currently 12 vols. Kassel u. Basel: Baerenreiter Verlag, and St. Louis: Concordia, 1955—. (In progress).

The following volumes are presently available:

1538   *Symphoniae iucundae (Mu 3)*
        Edited by Hans Albrecht. Foreword translated by Walter E. Buszin.

1539   *Officia paschali de resurrectione et ascensione Domini (Mu 8)*
        Edited by Robert L. Parker. English foreword.

1540   *Vesperarum precum officia (Mu 4)*
        Edited by Hans Joachim Moser. Foreword translated by Marie Hoyer Schroeder.

1541   Sixtus Dietrich, *Novum ac insigne opus musicum (Mu 7)*
        Edited by Walter E. Buszin. English foreword.

1543   Balthasar Resinarius, *Responsorum numero octoginta (Mu 1, 2)*
        Edited by Inge-Maria Schroeder. Foreword translated by Walter E. Buszin.

1544   *Postremum vespertini officii opus (Mu 5)*
        Edited by Paul G. Bunjes. English foreword.

1545   *Bicinia gallica, latina, germanica. Tomus I, II (Mu 6)*
        Edited by Bruce Bellingham. English foreword.

Other publications of Georg Rhau presently available include the following:

Sixtus Dietrich, *Hymnen*. Edited by Hermann Zenck with an introduction by Wilibald Gurlitt. St. Louis: Concordia, 1960. Introduction and preface in English translated by Theodore Hoelty-Nickel. (This is the 1545 collection *Novum opus musicum tres tomos*.)

Newe deudsche geistliche Gesenge . . . fuer die gemeinen Schulen (1544). (May be found in *Denkmaeler deutscher Tonkunst* [DdT], vol. 34.)

Selected References for Further Reading

Primary Sources:

Rhau, Georg. *Musikdrucke aus den Jahren 1538 bis 1545 in praktischer Neuausgabe.* General editor Hans Albrecht. Currently 12 vols. Kassel u. Basel: Baerenreiter Verlag, and St. Louis: Concordia, 1955—. (In progress).

————. *Enchiridion utriusque musicae practicae.* Facsimile edition. Edited by Hans Albrecht. Kassel u. Basel: Baerenreiter, 1951.

————. *Newe deudsche geistliche Gesenge.* Facsimile edition. 4 vols. Kassel u. Basel: Baerenreiter, 1969.

Secondary Sources:

Bellingham, Bruce A. *The* Biciniorum *in the Lutheran Latin Schools during the Reformation Period.* Ph.D. diss., University of Toronto, 1971.

Geck, Martin. "Rhau, Georg." Cols. 372–76 in vol. 11 of *Die Musik in Geschichte und Gegenwart.* Kassel u. Basel: Baerenreiter, 1963.

Mattfeld, Victor H. "Rhau, Georg." Pages 787–89 in vol. 15 of *The New Grove Dictionary of Music and Musicians.* Edited by Stanley Sadie. New York: Macmillan, 1980.

————. *Georg Rhaw's Publications for Vespers.* Musicological Studies XI. Brooklyn: Institute of Mediaeval Music, 1966.

Schrade, Leo. "The Editorial Practices of Georg Rhaw." Pages 32–42 in vol. 4 of *The Musical Heritage of the Church.* Edited by Theodore Hoelty-Nickel. St. Louis: Concordia, 1954.

4

Hans Leo Hassler

Herald of the Transition to the "New Style"

The musical style of the latter 15th and early 16th centuries, reflected in the compositions of Johann Walter and the publications of Georg Rhau, continued to set the model for Lutheran music in the first half of the 16th century. The first generation of Lutheran composers largely continued on the path set for them by the models of Josquin, Isaac, and Walter himself. The composers, both old and new, included in the various publications of Georg Rhau reflected both the spirit and the techniques of the masters of Flemish polyphony in which the polyphonic elaboration of the old church melodies in a variety of ways challenged the skill, craftsmanship, and art of the composer. Such a point of view was reinforced by the ideas of Luther, Walter, and others, who spoke often about the relationship between theology, the art of music, and music's place in the life of the worshiping community.

The second half of the 16th and the early 17th century saw the continuation of these general ideals reflected in the work of such composers as Joachim à Burck (1546–1610), Johannes Eccard (1553–1611), Christoph Demantius (1567–1643), Melchior Franck (ca. 1579–1639), and others who continued to reflect this earlier approach. But by the second half of the 16th century, new musical winds were beginning to blow, particularly from Italy, which were to have a significant impact on the development of music in the church of the Reformation. These new Italian innovations were to affect both Catholic and Lutheran composers alike. Among the more prominent Lutheran composers in whose work one begins to see the stirring of something new were Hans Leo Hassler (1562–1612), Adam Gumpeltzhaimer (ca. 1559–1625), Hieronymus Praetorius (1560–1629), Philippus Dulichius (1562–1631), and Michael Praetorius (1571–1621). It is to the life and contribution of Hans Leo Hassler that we now turn.

Hans Leo Hassler was born into a musical family. His father was an organist with a reputation as an eminent musician. While the exact date of Hassler's birth is uncertain, Hans Leo was baptized on October 26, 1564, the second son of Isaak Hassler (ca. 1530–1618), organist and musician of the town of Nuremberg. The Hassler family was known in Nuremberg already in the early 1400s. Hans Leo's grandfather, however, had settled for some time in the Joachimsthal in Bohemia. At that time, Isaak Hassler's teachers included Johann Matthesius, the first biographer of

Luther, and Nicolaus Herman, a teacher in the Latin school and cantor and organist in the local Lutheran church. Eventually the family returned to the family home in Nuremberg.

All three sons of Isaak Hassler—Kaspar (1562–1618), Hans Leo (1564–1612), and Jakob (1569–1622)—attained some degree of prominence in music. Kaspar, the oldest son, served a variety of churches in Nuremberg—St. Egidien, St. Lorenz, and St. Sebald—as organist from 1587 until his death. Jakob, the youngest son, served the Augsburg Fuggers as organist and later, having fallen into disgrace with the Fuggers, served as organist to Count Eitel Fritz of Hohenzollern at Hechingen. But it was Hans Leo, the middle son, who was to gain particular prominence and make a distinctive contribution to the development of music in Germany in the late 16th and early 17th centuries and to the music of the Lutheran church.

It is interesting to note that Hassler's life and work occurred at a time of great exploration, discovery, and general ferment throughout the world. In Europe the first compound microscope was made by Janssen in Holland (1590), Rembrandt was born (1606), and Galileo discovered the satellites of Jupiter (1610). In the New World, the colony of Jamestown was founded (1607) and Henry Hudson discovered the bay which would be named after him (1609). In Russia, Boris Gudunov became Czar after the death of Fedor, son of Ivan the Terrible (1598). The musical discovery and ferment which would result as a consequence of the young Hassler's visit to Italy in the 1580s would have an equally important impact on the future of German church music, an impact that would last well into the 18th century.

Hans Leo Hassler was born at a time when the preeminent musical style was that of Flemish polyphony. About the 1530s, Netherlands musicians also began to occupy a number of leading positions at various German courts. Such men as Petrus Maessens and Jacob Vaet (1529–67) went to Vienna; Mattheus le Maistre (ca. 1505–77) went to Dresden (where he succeeded Johann Walter as *Kapellmeister*); Adrian Coclico (ca. 1500–63) went to Koenigsberg and later to Nuremberg. But perhaps the most influential of all was Orlando di Lasso (1532–94) who went to the Bavarian court in Munich in 1556 and presided over a flourishing musical establishment. Through Leonhard Lechner (ca. 1550–1606), a boy chorister under di Lasso in Munich who later came to Nuremberg when Hassler was 13 years old, the influence of the international Flemish style made its impact on the young musician Hans Leo. But new musical developments in Italy were beginning to be felt throughout the musical world, and it would be Hassler's role to be the first important German

composer to travel to Italy and begin the century-long process of assimi-
lating into German music the spirit and technique of the developing Italian
Baroque style.

Although little is known of Hassler's early musical training, it was
most likely received from his father, Isaak. In the funeral sermon of Isaak
Hassler, it was said that he carefully brought up and trained his son Hans
Leo in the fear of God, in the free arts, and especially in the praiseworthy
art of music.

But other influences also undoubtedly affected young Hans Leo's
development. Prominent in Nuremberg during his formative years was
Leonhard Lechner, who had fervently committed to the Reformation
cause after converting from Catholicism at the age of 18. Lechner had
come to Nuremberg in 1575 from the Munich court chapel—where he had
served as a chorister under Orlando di Lasso—to serve as a teacher at the
St. Lorenz school in Nuremberg. While in Nuremberg, Lechner edited a
variety of volumes of motets and Masses of di Lasso and other masters
who were sung at the Bavarian court chapel. Lechner's activity in
Nuremberg as musician, composer, and editor undoubtedly provided
opportunity for the young Hassler to become acquainted with the work of
di Lasso, the master contrapuntalist of the day. The "di Lasso school" was
of great importance for Hans Leo. Even a casual perusal of his musical
work reflects his continuing debt to this great contrapuntal tradition.

Hassler at Venice (1584–85)

In 1584—the same year that Lechner left Nuremberg—the 22-year-old
Hans Leo Hassler left his home city of Nuremberg to journey to the colorful and cosmopolitan city of Venice for the purpose of advancing his
musical study. It is interesting to observe that it was Venice, not the more
musically provincial and conservative Rome, which attracted young
Hassler. Nuremberg at this time had close commercial ties with Venice,
and such a journey was a logical consequence of those ties. While the circumstances surrounding the details of the trip are not clear, it is entirely
possible that Hassler went to Venice at the expense of the Nuremberg
town council.

Among the leading musicians at Venice at the time of Hassler's visit
were Andrea Gabrieli (ca. 1520–86), first organist at St. Mark's cathedral,
and Gioseffo Zarlino (1517–90), prominent musical theorist and composer. Hassler's study was with Andrea Gabrieli. While there, Hassler also
became acquainted with Giovanni Gabrieli (ca. 1554–1612), a fellow student and nephew of Andrea, an acquaintance that developed into a life-

long friendship.[1] Other Italian composers whose works Hassler undoubtedly knew were Orfeo Vecchi (1540–1603), Giovanni Gastoldi (?–1622), and Claudio Merulo (1533–1604), as some of his later compositions seem to suggest.

The center of music-making in Venice was the cathedral of St. Mark. At the time Hassler studied at the cathedral, its history included such important musicians as Adrian Willaert (ca. 1490–1562), Andrea Gabrieli, and Claudio Merulo. Some years later, musicians such as Giovanni Gabrieli—Hassler's fellow student—and Claudio Monteverdi would be active there. Characteristic of the musical developments which drew on

Fig. 4. Hans Leo Hassler

the unique architecture of St. Mark's cathedral was the use of *cori spezzati* (broken choir)—the use of a variety of contrasting choirs of voices and instruments, echo effects, and a more progressive use of instruments. All this sound in the spacious and acoustically hospitable environment of St. Mark's produced an effect that engulfed the listener in sensuous sound, an experience that stood in conspicuous contrast to the more austere character of German polyphonic music.

In addition, Italian developments related to the secular madrigal, the *villanella*, the *balletto*, and similar forms opened up to Hassler the vitality, exuberance, elegance, and lyric grace which were quite new to his Germanic background. Hassler studied, absorbed, worked at his composition, and in general luxuriated in the music of Venice for 18 months. It was an experience which was to bear increasing fruit on his composition and would have a significant influence on the future course of German church music.[2]

Hassler at Augsburg (1585–1601)

In March 1585, Hassler left Venice briefly to go to Augsburg to play

---

[1] The *Reliquiae sacrorum concentuum* (Nuremberg, 1615), an anthology of works by both Giovanni Gabrieli and Hassler, was published posthumously by Georg Gruber, a Nuremberg merchant who lived in Venice in 1600 and for whom Gabrieli and Hassler had each composed a wedding motet.

[2] From the time of Hassler to that of Handel and Mozart, many German composers traditionally sought their final education in Italy. See Manfred F. Bukofzer, *Music in the Baroque Era* (New York: W. W. Norton & Co., 1947), 83.

for the wedding of a member of the wealthy Fugger family, a family important in the business and banking world of the day. The Gabrielis had close contact with the Fugger family, and it is not impossible that Hassler was recommended to the Fuggers by the Gabrielis for employment. In January 1586, Hassler ended his stay in Venice and returned to Augsburg, where he took up a position as organist to Octavian (II) Fugger, the great merchant prince, banker, and patron of the arts. The Fuggers apparently had no problem with the fact that Hassler was an adherent of the Reformation faith.[3] For more than a century, beginning with the first Jakob Fugger (1459–1525), the Fugger family "lavished wealth, enthusiasm, discernment on building their native town as a cultural center. Churches were built or enlarged and refurbished; organs were commissioned and built for them; the finest singers, composers, and organists were brought and maintained in their service."[4]

The importance of Augsburg in the latter 15th and early 16th centuries was enhanced through the frequent presence of Maximilian I, emperor of the Holy Roman Empire (1493–1519), who transferred the *Hofkapelle* to Augsburg in 1492 and, over the years, assembled a noted group of musicians—among them Paul Hofhaimer, Heinrich Isaac, and Ludwig Senfl—as organists and singers. A famous woodcut by Hans Weiditz dated 1519 shows Maximilian worshiping in the *Annakirche* in Augsburg. This church would—following the Diet of Augsburg in 1518—become "a principal bastion of Lutheran activity and, only a little later, a fountain of musical and scholastic development for the new faith."[5] That the emperor's *Hofkapelle* sang with some frequency at the *Annakirche* may be assumed because of the location of the Fugger Chapel at the west end of the church—a chapel endowed in 1509 in an agreement between the Fugger brothers, Jakob and Ulrich, and Johannes Fortis, prior of the Carmelite cloister at St. Anna. An especially fine organ for this chapel, commissioned by the Fuggers and dating from 1512, was built by Jehan Behaim of Dubrau. Adam Gumpeltzhaimer, who became cantor and preceptor at the *Annakirche* in 1581, only five years before Hassler arrived in Augsburg, was the most prominent musician, composer, and scholar to be associated with the *Annakirche* in the latter decades of the 16th century.

Although Hassler was a Lutheran serving at a Catholic court, his years

---

[3] Gustav Reese notes that "Hassler seems to have been a Protestant." See *Music in the Renaissance* (rev. ed; New York: W. W. Norton & Co., 1959), 687.

[4] Louise E. Cuyler, "Musical Activity in Augsburg and Its Annakirche, ca. 1470–1630," in *Cantors at the Crossroads: Essays on Church Music in Honor of Walter E. Buszin* (ed. Johannes Riedel; St. Louis: Concordia, 1967), 35.

[5] Ibid., op. cit., 41.

Fig. 5. Maximilian I worshiping in the *Annakirche* in Augsburg (1519)

in Augsburg were his most productive, and with his establishment in Augsburg, Hassler's fame soon spread throughout Germany. In 1595, the emperor knighted Hassler and his two brothers.

Hassler's years in Augsburg saw the publication of a number of individual works and collections which reflected his study in Venice, as well as the continuing influence of the di Lasso school of composers that had been influential in his early training. In 1588 two single motets—"Laudate Dominum" and "Nuptiae factae sunt"—were included in a collection published by Frederick Lindner, a Nuremberg editor. In 1590 a collection of 24 Italian secular songs for four voices, *Canzonette*, was published. The following year (1591) saw the appearance of the *Cantiones sacrae*, a collection of 39 polyphonic motets for four to 12 voices. In 1596 the *Neue teutsche Gesang nach Art der welschen Madrigalien und Canzonetten* for four to eight voices appeared; in the same year, Hassler's *Madrigali*, Italian madrigals for five to eight voices, also appeared. Hassler was—together with Leonhard Lechner and, later, Heinrich Schuetz—among the few German composers who wrote secular music on Italian texts. In 1599 Hassler's *Missae*, a set of eight Masses for four to eight voices appeared; they were undoubtedly written for use in the Catholic services at Augsburg. Hassler's first Mass is a parody Mass on the motet "Dixit Maria." The beginning of the Kyrie follows (Ex. 15).

Ex. 15. Hans Leo Hassler, "Kyrie" from Mass I in *Missae* (1599)

In 1601 Hassler's *Lustgarten neuer teutscher Gesaeng* was published in Nuremberg. It contains 39 secular German songs in *gagliarda* and *balletto* style together with 12 instrumental intradas for six string or wind instruments without *continuo*. The set of intradas from the *Lustgarten neuer teutscher Gesaeng* are particularly interesting as instrumental pieces in their own right. Such examples of independent wind music, pioneered by the two Gabrielis in Venice and of which Hassler was one of the earliest composers, were undoubtedly ideal for use as festive processional music and for preludes at a variety of church celebrations, pageants, and municipal gatherings (Ex. 16).

Ex. 16. Hans Leo Hassler, "Intrada" from the *Lustgarten neuer teutscher Gesaeng* (1601)

Undoubtedly the most famous song from this collection is the five-voice setting of a secular love song "Mein G'muet ist mir verwirret." Hassler set this text—a five-stanza acrostic poem spelling out the name Maria—to an original tune which subsequently appeared in 1613 adapted to the words "Herzlich tut mich verlangen." Johann Crueger included the tune in his *Praxis pietatis melica* (1647) to the words "O Haupt voll Blut und Wunden," an association employed by Johann Sebastian Bach in his *St. Matthew Passion* and which continues to this day. The original version of this setting repeated the final phrase of the music, a repetition which did not survive its transformation into one of the best known Passion hymns of the church (Ex. 17). Another important collection of Hassler from 1601 was the *Sacri concentus,* which contains 52 motets for four to 12 voices,

Ex. 17. Hans Leo Hassler, "Mein G'muet ist mir verwirret" from *Lustgarten neuer teutscher Gesaeng* (1601)

enlarged in 1612 to 63 motets together with three instrumental works. This collection clearly reflects the influence of his time in Venice with its use of multiple choirs and antiphonal effects (Ex. 18). The years at Augsburg were musically productive indeed for Hassler.

Ex. 18. Hans Leo Hassler, "Laudate Dominum" from *Sacri concentus* (1601)

The years at Augsburg were also busy in other ways. Hassler received an invitation from Heinrich Julius, Herzog of Braunschweig, to participate, along with 50 other famous organists and organ builders, in the 1596 dedication of the famous organ in the castle church at Groeningen near Halberstadt. Hassler's brother Kaspar and Michael Praetorius were also among the guests at this occasion. In 1597 Moritz, Landgrave of Hesse, like the Fuggers a generous patron of the arts, sought to obtain Hassler's service at his court at Kassel, but because Hassler was still under obligation to the Fuggers, nothing more came of this.

As early as his years in Augsburg, and also later in Nuremberg, Hassler became involved in the manufacture of mechanical instruments and musical clocks. This business venture and the many problems which ensued—he was often involved in legal disputes with his competitors—took up much of his time.[6] A fine engraving showing the aristocratic young Hassler from the time when he served as organist to the Fuggers is extant, made by Domenicus Custos, Augsburg, 1593.

Hassler at Nuremberg (1601–04) and Ulm (1605–08)

In 1600 Octavian (II) Fugger died, leaving Hassler temporarily unemployed. He immediately applied for and received an appointment as director of the town band at Augsburg, but shortly after, on August 16, 1601, Hassler accepted an offer to become the chief musician of Nuremberg, leaving Augsburg on December 6, 1601. While at Nuremberg, Hassler was also appointed honorary organist (*Hof-Diener* and *Kammer Organist*) at the court of Rudolf II in Prague, a largely sinecure appointment, a position which required little or no work but provided some compensation.

In 1604 the Nuremberg council gave Hassler permission for a leave of absence to go to Ulm where he subsequently married Cordula Claus in 1605, a marriage that remained childless. That same year Hassler gave notice to the Nuremberg council of his intent to remain at Ulm where, in 1607, he became a citizen. Hassler settled in Ulm for several years.

In these latter years of his life, Hassler prepared the only two collections specifically designed for use in Lutheran services. Under commission from the city of Nuremberg and the strictly Lutheran Elector Christian II of Dresden, Hassler prepared his *Psalmen und christliche Gesaenge, mit vier Stimmen auf die Melodien fugweis componirt* (1607),[7] and his *Kirchengesaenge: Psalmen und geistliche Lieder auf die gemeinen Melodien mit vier Stimmen simpliciter gesetzt* of 1608. The *Psalmen . . . fugweis componirt* (*fugweis* meaning "in the fugal style") was dedicated to Elector Christian II of Saxony. It contains 52 settings of 30 chorale melodies in elaborate polyphonic chorale-motet style in which each of the voices participates in the melodic contours of the chorale.

---

[6] Walter Buszin notes that "while organist at the Collegiate Institute of St. Moritz in Augsburg [Hassler] devoted much of his time and effort to the planning and erection of its large mechanical organ and to lavish lawsuits which were levied against him by his competitors in connection with this project." See Walter E. Buszin, "Lutheran Church Music in the Age of Classical Lutheran Theology: Hans Leo Hassler and Michael Praetorius," in vol. 1 of *The Symposium on 17th Century Lutheranism* (ed. by A. C. Piepkorn, Robert Preus, and Erwin Luecker; St. Louis: Concordia, 1962), 62–76.

[7] This collection was particularly important both musically and liturgically. It was part of a group of collections revived in the 18th century and re-edited by Kirnberger, a pupil of Johann Sebastian Bach.

From this collection, the setting of "Nun freut euch lieben Christen ge'mein" (Ex. 19) clearly illustrates Hassler's mastery of the old polyphonic style. The *Kirchengesaenge . . . simpliciter gesetzt* was dedi-

Ex. 19. Hans Leo Hassler, "Nun freut euch lieben Christen ge'mein" from *Psalmen . . . fugweis componirt* (1607)

cated to the city of Nuremberg and contained 71 settings in cantional style, the melody appearing in the upper voice, all the voices proceeding in similar rhythm. The simple, straightforward setting of the chorale melody "Vom Himmel hoch da komm ich her" (Ex. 20) exemplifies this practice. The chorales of this collection represent essentially the old chorale repertoire established in the *de tempore* hymn cycle. This collection is usually regarded as representing the highpoint in the development of the South German cantional collections. In the *Kirchengesaenge . . . simpliciter gesetzt*, in a sense his final testament, Hassler included several settings in eight parts for two choirs. The first of these is the particularly touching setting of "Herzlich Lieb hab ich dich, O Herr"—a relatively simple work for two choirs which sing the three stanzas of the chorale antiphonally. This piece continues to find a place in the repertoire of many Lutheran choirs. In these two collections, one can see the two ways in which the Lutheran chorale melodies would develop in the coming decades: simple cantional style—already seen in embryonic fashion in several settings by Johann Walter and which would be developed further in the 17th century by such composers as Praetorius, Schein, Scheidt, and Schuetz—and the polyphonic motet style.

Ex. 20. Hans Leo Hassler, "Vom Himmel hoch da komm ich her"
from *Kirchengesaenge . . . simpliciter gesetzt* (1608)

Hassler at Dresden (1608–12)

In 1608 Hassler left Ulm to go to Dresden where he had applied for
and received an appointment as organist to the Electoral Chapel. Soon
after settling in Dresden, he contracted tuberculosis, which proved incur-
able. Throughout the last years of his life, Hassler was plagued by this ill-
ness. On a journey to Frankfurt in the company of the Elector of Saxony,
who was attending an imperial election, Hassler died on June 8, 1612, at
the age of 47. He was buried in Frankfurt am Main on June 10, 1612. His
burial sermon was delivered by the court preacher, Daniel Haenichen.
Following Hassler's death, his duties at the Electoral Chapel were taken
over by Michael Praetorius and Heinrich Schuetz.

While Hassler's reputation in his lifetime was largely a result of his
work as organist, only a small amount of organ music by Hassler is extant.
It consists chiefly of ricercare, canzona, and versets designed for use in
the Catholic service. Although he was an organist throughout his career,

Hassler organ works are probably the least original of his compositions. Largely following the example of the organ works of Andrea and Giovanni Gabrieli and typical of the late Renaissance, many of his organ compositions tend toward the utmost pomp and splendor.[8] The Agnus Dei (Ex. 21) reflects the florid, coloristic effects which may be seen as well in the organ intonations of Giovanni Gabrieli. The use of Reformation melodies may be seen in his treatment of Luther's "Wir glauben all an einem Gott," which carries the melody in the upper voice in slightly orna- mented long notes against a highly coloristic accompaniment (Ex. 22).[9]

Ex. 21. Hans Leo Hassler, Agnus Dei for organ

Ex. 22. Hans Leo Hassler, "Wir glauben all an einem Gott" for organ

The posthumous collection *Venusgarten oder neue lustige liebliche Taenz* for four to six voices (Nuremberg, 1615), which included 13 pieces reprinted from the *Neue teutsche Gesang*, should also be mentioned, as well as several other works scattered throughout a number of other publi- cations. Of particular interest is Hassler's setting of the *Litany Teusch Herrn Dr. Martini Lutheri* for seven voices (Nuremberg, 1619).

Hassler was a transitional figure who, in his journey to Italy, foreshad- owed the growing importance and influence of Italian musical develop- ments in German music of the 17th century. He was less an innovator than he was a developer of the new musical ideas flowing from Italy. In his sacred music, particularly in his Latin Masses and motets, he remained largely the practitioner of the *style antico* or *prima prattica*, as the old polyphonic style came to be called. Yet this is not completely so. For if the

---

[8] See Willi Apel, "Solo Instrumental Music," in *The Age of Humanism 1540–1630* (ed. Gerald Abraham; vol. IV of *The New Oxford History of Music;* London: Oxford University Press, 1968), 659.

[9] Examples of Hassler's organ works may be seen in Hans Leo Hassler, *Ordinarium et proprium de apostolis. Versetti e corali per organo* (ed. Oscar Mischiati; Paideia Brescia & Baerenreiter Kassel, n.d.).

roots of Hassler's many works for more than one choir can be traced to antecedents in the works of di Lasso and others of the Flemish tradition, they also reflect something of the newer polychoral style of the Venetian school. If in his *Psalmen . . . fugweis componirt* Hassler reflects a classic example of the all-pervasiveness of polyphony as each voice participates in the melodic contours of the chorale, in his *Lustgarten* he "transplanted to German soil the villanelle, canzonette, and dance songs of Gastoldi and Vecchi."[10] If in his *Kirchengesaenge . . . simpliciter gesetzt* he reaffirmed the old chorales with his simple homorhythmic settings, in his keyboard music Hassler "preserved the tradition of the colorists . . . and leaned heavily on the Italian models."[11] Among the many indications of his more lasting influence was the inclusion of many of Hassler's compositions in some of the most important anthologies of the day, notably Erhard Bodenschatz's *Florilegium selectissimorum cantionum* (1603),[12] copies of which were still in use in Leipzig at the time of Johann Sebastian Bach.[13]

Hassler was a rare phenomenon in late 16th-century Lutheran music. He was essentially a practical musician and an organist by profession. His training as a cantor was not academic, unlike many of the great figures of his day, yet he was thoroughly skilled in the art and craft of the music of his time. Yet Hassler moved beyond the limitations of the academic to a broader culture, exemplified not only in the various kinds of music he composed, but in his general lifestyle and in his various business undertakings. The characterization of him by his native town of Nuremberg as *Musicus inter Germanos sua aetate summus* ("a musician whose like has not been found among the Germans of his time") was surely deserved.

If Hassler was the first of the great German composers to reflect the new mood of the Italian Baroque, the greater flowering of that spirit was yet to come. Hassler opened the door for the new breezes blowing from the south. It remained open for such men as Michael Praetorius, Johann Hermann Schein, Samuel Scheidt, and ultimately Heinrich Schuetz to explore the further dimensions of this new music. In so doing, they moved German church music into paths which would ultimately culminate in the music of Johann Sebastian Bach.

---

[10] Bukofzer, op. cit., 98.

[11] Ibid., 104. In Bukofzer's view, Hassler's songs represented a hybrid vocal-instrumental literature in which the *continuo* was either optional or lacking altogether, characteristic of this period of transition.

[12] A revised edition of 1618 appeared with the title *Florilegium Portense*. Together with a second part which appeared in 1621, it had a rather permanent place in the Lutheran churches and schools of the period.

[13] This collection "had a hundred years' tradition in the choir of St. Thomas." Arnold Schering as quoted in Guenther Stiller, *Johann Sebastian Bach and Liturgical Life in Leipzig* (St. Louis: Concordia, 1984), 86.

1560 1570 1580 1590 1600 1610 1620

HANS LEO HASSLER

Canzonette (1590)

Cantiones sacrae (1591)

Neue teutsche Gesang (1596)
Madrigali (1596)

Missae (1599)

Sacri concentus (1601)
Lustgarten neuer teutscher Gesaeng (1601)

Psalmen . . . fugweis componirt (1607)

Kirchengesaenge . . . simpliciter gesetzt (1608)

Guide to Hans Leo Hassler's Collected Works

Hans Leo Hassler, *Saemtliche Werke* (*SW*). Edited by C. Russell Crosby Jr. Currently 10 vols. Wiesbaden: Breitkopf u. Haertel, 1961—. (In progress).

The following volumes are presently available:

1590   *Canzonette* (*SW* 2)
          A collection of 24 Italian secular songs for four voices written in largely homophonic texture.

1591   *Cantiones sacrae* (*SW* 1)
          A collection of 39 polyphonic motets for four to 12 voices, expanded in later editions (1597, 1607) to 48 motets, including two Magnificats for four voices. Included are 15 motets for four voices, 13 for five voices, eight for six voices, one for seven voices, seven for eight voices, one for 10 voices, one for 11 voices, and two for 12 voices. The settings for seven and more voices are arranged for two or three choirs.

1596   *Neue teutsche Gesang nach Art der welschen Madrigalien und Canzonetten* (*SW* 2)
          Twenty-four madrigals and canzonetta for four to eight voices. Included are eight for four voices, seven for five voices, seven for six voices, and two for eight voices in two choirs.

          Madrigali (SW 3)
          A set of 33 Italian madrigals. Included are 16 for five voices, 12 for six voices, one for seven voices, and four for eight voices. The pieces for seven and eight voices are set for two choirs.

1599   *Missae* (*SW* 4)
          A set of eight Masses for four to eight voices. Included are three Masses for four voices, two for five voices, two for six voices, and one Mass for eight voices for two choirs.

1601   *Sacri concentus* (*SW* 5, 6)

The first edition contained 52 motets for four to 12 voices including instrumental canzonas. Enlarged in 1612 to 63 motets and three instrumental works. Included are 13 works for four voices, 11 for five voices, 12 for six voices, and two for seven voices. Pieces for two choirs include 19 motets for eight voices, one for nine voices, and three for 10 voices. Two motets are included for 12 voices for three choirs. The instrumental works include two canzonas and one ricercare.

Lustgarten neuer teutscher Gesaeng (*SW* 9)

Includes 39 secular German songs in the style of *balleti* and *gagliarda* for four to eight voices, plus 12 instrumental intradas written for six instruments. In this collection is found the five-part setting of "Mein G'muet ist mir verwirret" to the tune that ultimately became associated with the text "O sacred head now wounded."

1607   *Psalmen und christliche Gesaenge mit vier Stimmen auf die Melodien fugweis componirt* (*SW* 7)

Fifty-two settings of 30 chorale melodies in chorale-motet style for four voices.

1608   *Kirchengesaenge: Psalmen und geistliche Lieder auf die gemeinen Melodien mit vier Stimmen simpliciter gesetzt* (*SW* 8)

Seventy-one settings of chorale melodies in simple cantional style. Sixty-seven settings are for four voices, four settings for eight voices in two choirs.

Vokalwerke aus zeitgenoessische Drucken (*SW* 10)

Various works including one for four voices, three for five voices, five for six voices, the *Litany Teusch* for seven voices, eight for eight voices, plus two additional works for six voices.

Vokalwerke aus zeitgenoessische Drucken (*SW* 11)

Various multichorus works, including three for 12 voices, one for 13 voices, one for 15 voices, two for 16 voices, one for 18 voices, and a *Missa* (*sine nomine*) for 12 voices.

For Hassler's works for organ and keyboard, see *H. L. Hassler: Werke fuer Orgel und Klavier.* Edited by E. von Werra. DTB. vii, Jg. Iv/2 (1903).

Selected References for Further Reading

Primary Source:

Hans Leo Hassler, *Saemtliche Werke.* Edited by C. Russell Crosby Jr. Currently 10 vols. Wiesbaden: Breitkopf u. Haertel, 1961—. (In progress).

Secondary Sources:

Blankenburg, Walter. "Hans Leo Hassler." Pages 294–97 in vol. 8 of *The New Grove Dictionary of Music and Musicians.* Edited by Stanley Sadie. New York: Macmillan, 1980.

Buszin, Walter E. "Lutheran Church Music in the Age of Classical Lutheran Theology: Hans Leo Hassler and Michael Praetorius." Pages 62–76 in vol. 1 of *The Symposium on 17th Century Lutheranism.* Edited by A. C. Piepkorn, Robert Preus, and Erwin Luecker. St. Louis: Concordia, 1962.

Cuyler, Louise E. "Musical Activity in Augsburg and Its Annakirche, ca. 1470–1630." Pages 33–43 in *Cantors at the Crossroads: Essays on Church Music in Honor of Walter E. Buszin.* Edited by Johannes Riedel. St. Louis: Concordia, 1967.

Panetta, Vincent J. "Hans Leo Hassler and the Keyboard Toccata: Antecedents, Sources, Style." Ph.D. diss., Harvard University, 1991.

Wagner, Rudolf, and Friedrich Blume."Hassler, Hans Leo." Cols. 1798–1813 in vol. 5 of *Die Musik in Geschichte und Gegenwart.* Kassel u. Basel: Baerenreiter, 1956.

5

Michael Praetorius

Conservator of the Chorale

It is difficult to overestimate the importance of the life and work of Michael Praetorius (1571–1621) in the shaping of the Lutheran

musical tradition of the late 16th and early 17th centuries. Born almost at the midpoint between the birth of Martin Luther and the death of Heinrich Schuetz, Praetorius is particularly significant in shaping the early Lutheran musical heritage as it moved from the Renaissance into the emerging Baroque. With one foot planted firmly in the Renaissance and its musical tradition and the other stepping boldly into a musical future which was still emerging, Praetorius' served as a mediator between the two for the Lutheran tradition. As one whose life bridged the transition from the 16th to the 17th

Fig. 6. Michael Praetorius

century, Praetorius' life and music demonstrated a remarkable and firm commitment to the heritage of the Reformation and simultaneously reflected an openness to developing changes in musical style. His affirmation of tradition—reflected particularly in his ceaseless efforts to preserve the chorale for future generations and in his constant labors to encourage and provide extensive musical material for the practice of alternation in hymn singing (*alternatim praxis*)—and his openness to the future—demonstrated in his vigorous appropriation of the Venetian polychoral tradition as well as, especially in his later works, the use of figured bass and his employment of the Italian style of singing—were the two touchstones of his contribution to Lutheran music. Praetorius has been characterized as one who was "positively obsessed by the Lutheran hymn, yet who devoted a great part of his tremendous creative energy to the absorption of every Italian innovation and its fusion with his own characteristically vernacular type of sacred music."[1] The one Italian innovation

---

[1] Hans Redlich, "Early Baroque Church Music," in *The Age of Humanism 1540–1630* (ed. Gerald Abraham; vol. IV of *The New Oxford History of Music*; London: Oxford University Press, 1968), 546.

of the time which Praetorius did not take up was the recitative, with the result that his music manifests an austerity and sobriety more characteristic of the 16th than the 17th century.

Praetorius' direct familial connection and acquaintance with the early Reformation and its music, together with his underlying concern that church music be solidly rooted and grounded in theology, make him typical of the Lutheran cantor of his time. But whatever forms his music employed, and they were many and varied, it was always the Lutheran chorale which was its generating force and which was at the heart and center of his life and work.

Michael Praetorius was born on February 15, 1571,[2] in Creuzburg on the Werra River near Eisenach. He was the son of Michael Schultheiss[3] who had come from Bunzlau in Silesia. Michael Praetorius' father was a teacher at the famous Latin School in Torgau, where he was a colleague of Johann Walter, the first cantor of the Lutheran church.

Early Life

After a period of theological study in Wittenberg with Luther and Melanchthon, Michael's father became a pastor. As an orthodox Lutheran, he became involved in the theological strife which overtook Lutheranism in the years following Luther's death, a situation which ultimately led to his giving up the ministry. One of his charges was in the town of Creuzburg where he served from 1569 to 1573 and where his son Michael was born.[4] After trouble broke out in Creuzburg, the family moved to Torgau where young Michael attended the Latin school where his father had previously taught and where the cantor was Michael Vogt, a pupil of Johann Walter and Walter's successor.

In 1583 Michael matriculated at the University of Frankfurt on the Oder River where his brother Andreas taught theology. However, Michael was apparently too young, and he first attended school at Zerbst where two of his sisters lived. Eventually he returned to Frankfurt where he studied philosophy and theology. Following the death of his brother Andreas,

---

[2] While the date is not completely certain, this is the date given in the biography of Praetorius in Johann Walther's *Musikalisches Lexicon* (1732) and is generally accepted. See the facs. ed. (Kassel u. Basel: Baerenreiter Verlag, 1953), 491.

[3] The family name was apparently Schultheiss or Schultze, the name Praetorius likely had been taken as the result of what was then a fashion for Latinizing family names. The German word *Schultheiss* meant a village mayor; the Latin *Praetorius* was the term for a civic leader.

[4] Praetorius often signed his name with the initials *M.P.C.* referring to his birthplace— *Michael Praetorius Creuzburgensis*. He also associated these initials with the Latin phrase *Mihi Patria Coelum* ("For me, my homeland is heaven").

upon whom he was dependent for his subsistence, in 1586 Michael became organist at the church of St. Mary, the university and parish church of Frankfurt. Despite no systematic musical training prior to this appointment, Michael retained this post—according to his own account—for three years while continuing his studies.

In the Service of Duke Heinrich Julius—
Groeningen and Wolfenbuettel

It is not clear why Praetorius gave up his post at St. Mary's in Frankfurt, but he apparently settled in Wolfenbuettel in the early 1590s. In 1595—again according to his own account in the *Motectae et psalmi latini* (1607) and the *Polyhymnia caduceatrix* (1619)—he entered the service of the young Duke Heinrich Julius of Brunswick-Wolfenbuettel, whom he served as organist. Praetorius was to remain in the service of Duke Heinrich Julius until the duke's death in 1613. In the fall of 1596 when the famous organ built by David Beck—of the well-known German family of organ builders—for the chapel of the castle at Groeningen near Halberstadt was dedicated, Praetorius was among some 50 famous organists and organ builders of Germany who were invited to attend. The castle—together with its chapel and organ—had been built by Heinrich Julius as bishop after introducing the Reformation there in 1591. The many famous musicians in attendance at this occasion included Hieronymus Praetorius, Hans Leo Hassler, Kaspar Hassler, and Heinrich Compenius, at which time Michael Praetorius became personally acquainted with them.

In 1603 Praetorius married Anna Lachemacher from Halberstadt, a union which bore him two sons—Michael in 1604 and Ernst in 1606. Praetorius was apparently held in such high esteem that in 1604—in addition to retaining the post of court organist—he was made court *Kapellmeister* following the retirement of his predecessor Thomas Mancinus.[5] Praetorius remained as organist in both Wolfenbuettel and Groeningen. Under the patronage and protection of Duke Heinrich Julius, Praetorius established himself in the years following as the leading Lutheran *Kapellmeister* and composer of Germany.

The years in Wolfenbuettel were ones of industrious musical activity for Praetorius. During this period, he published a number of particularly noteworthy collections: the *Musae Sioniae* (1605–1610); a number of

---

[5] Thomas Mancinus (1550–1611/12) served as *Kapellmeister* at Groeningen and in 1587, at the invitation of Duke Julius, founded the Wolfenbuettel *Hofkantorei*—which, under the reign of Duke Heinrich Julius, became one of the leading musical groups in Germany. Mancinus directed the choir until his retirement in 1604.

Latin liturgical works under the general title of *Leiturgodia* (1607, 1611); a collection of dances called *Terpsichore* (1612), the only part of a larger project—the *Musae aoniae*—which Praetorius envisioned as a secular counterpart to the *Musae Sioniae*; and *Urania* (1613), a collection of polychoral settings of chorales for two to four choirs.

His first published work, the *Musae Sioniae*, published in nine parts from 1605 to 1610, is in many ways the cornerstone of Praetorius' output. It has been described as "a veritable encyclopedia of chorale arrangement."[6] This collection consisted of some 1,244 compositions ranging from overwhelming polychoral settings of the standard chorales that clearly reflected his acquaintance with and indebtedness to the Venetian style (Parts I–IV) to simple harmonizations in cantional style (Parts V–IX). Ex. 23 from Part I of the *Musae Sioniae* based on the chorale "Allein Gott in der Höh sei Ehr" reflects Praetorius' early use of the polychoral style.

---

[6] Manfred F. Bukofzer, *Music in the Baroque Era* (New York: W. W. Norton & Co., 1947), 84.

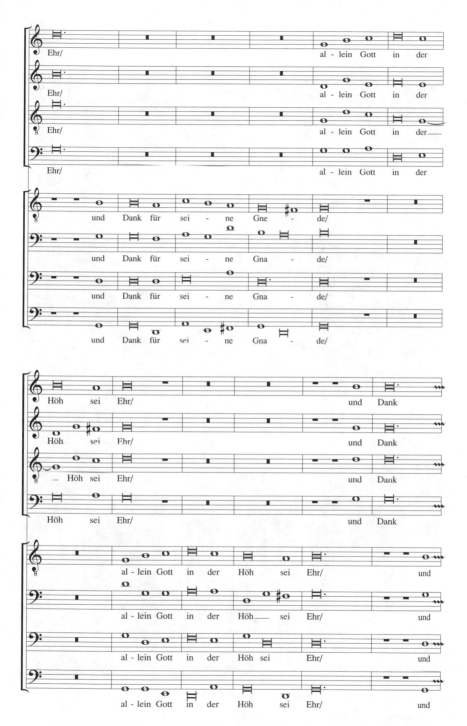

Ex. 23. Michael Praetorius, "Allein Gott in der Höh sei Ehr" from *Musae Sioniae Part I* (1605)

Fig. 7. Woodcut from Praetorius' works

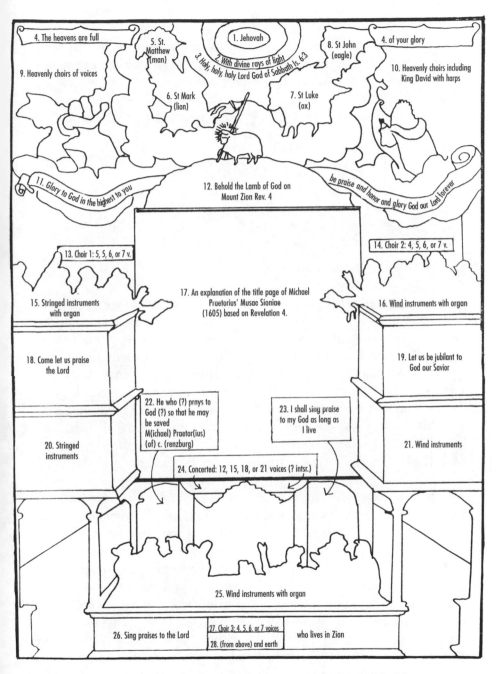

1. Jehovah
2. With divine rays of light
3. Holy, holy, holy Lord God of Sabbath Is. 6:3
4. The heavens are full
4. of your glory
5. St. Matthew (man)
6. St Mark (lion)
7. St Luke (ox)
8. St John (eagle)
9. Heavenly choirs of voices
10. Heavenly choirs including King David with harps
11. Glory to God in the highest to you
be praise and honor and glory God our Lord forever
12. Behold the Lamb of God on Mount Zion Rev. 4
13. Choir 1: 5, 5, 6, or 7 v.
14. Choir 2: 4, 5, 6, or 7 v.
15. Stringed instruments with organ
16. Wind instruments with organ
17. An explanation of the title page of Michael Praetorius' Musae Sioniae (1605) based on Revelation 4.
18. Come let us praise the Lord
19. Let us be jubilant to God our Savior
20. Stringed instruments
21. Wind instruments
22. He who (?) prays to God (?) so that he may be saved M(ichael) Praetor(ius) (of) c. (renzburg)
23. I shall sing praise to my God as long as I live
24. Concerted: 12, 15, 18, or 21 voices (? intsr.)
25. Wind instruments with organ
26. Sing praises to the Lord
27. Choir 3: 4, 5, 6, or 7 voices
28. (from above) and earth
who lives in Zion

Fig. 7a. Explanation of woodcut (Courtesy of Carlos Messerli and Gerhard Krodel)

Ex. 24, a setting of "Nun komm, der Heiden Heiland," reflects Praetorius' simple cantional-style settings. In Part IX of *Musae Sioniae,* Praetorius distinguishes between three ways of presenting the chorale: "motet-wise" ("Auff Muteten Art"), in which the chorale pervaded the contrapuntal interplay of all the voices, much in the manner of the customary motet style; "madrigal-wise" ("Madrigalisch"), in which the chorale was broken into small fragments and motives set in concertato dialogue; and *"cantus-firmus*-wise" ("vom Autore erst erfundene Art") in

Ex. 24. Michael Praetorius, "Nun komm, der Heiden Heiland" from *Musae Sioniae Part V* (1607)

which the *cantus firmus* was left intact and led against various *ostinato* motives. While these categories are not always clearly indistinguishable, the first and the third belonged to the general category of the chorale motet, the second demonstrating Praetorius' development toward the chorale concertato. Part IX of the *Musae Sioniae* also includes some tentative experimentation with *basso continuo* and the concertato style, experiments that would be enlarged upon and developed more thoroughly in his *Polyhymnia.* The *Musae Sioniae* not only reflects the great variety of types of settings Praetorius employed, it also demonstrates the attractiveness of Praetorius' music, shown in the continuing appeal of his simple four-part setting of "Es ist ein Ros'entsprungen."

The title page of Praetorius' *Musae Sioniae Part I* (1605) clearly reflects the late Renaissance practice of voices and instruments joining together, as well as points to the influence of the Venetian practice of locating various choirs in the different balconies or other spaces of the church. In addition, this woodcut clearly reflects the understanding that both heaven and earth, voices and instruments, join together in the praise of God. At the top left and right of the illustration are the words "The heavens are full . . . of your glory" as reflected in the heavenly choirs, instruments, the four Evangelists, all gathered around Jehovah's throne. At the bottom of the page are the words " . . . and earth," reflecting the entire cosmos joined in praise of its creator. This particular woodcut was used in a number of Praetorius' other publications as well. It is worth particular study.

The *Musae Sioniae* reflects an amazingly wide range of musical settings, all of them, however, based on the Lutheran chorale, which would remain at the heart of Praetorius' work. The *Musae Sioniae* also reflects Praetorius' deep concern for the theological and musical tradition of the Reformation church. At the beginning of the collection, he includes Johann Walter's German translation of Luther's "Encomion musices," the Latin preface to the *Symphonia iucundae*. It stands at the head of this comprehensive collection as a tribute to the first cantor of the Lutheran church as well as an affirmation of its theological content. Praetorius also included several of Walter's compositions in Parts 5 and 7 of the *Musae Sioniae* and quoted in the *Syntagma musicum* Walter's recollections of his work with Luther in developing the music for the *Deudsche Messe*. Each of these details reflects Praetorius' view of the theological and musical tradition of the Lutheran church not as a quaint relic of the past, but as a living force and a solid foundation on which any vitality in the church's life and worship must inevitably build.

Of the Latin liturgical works, grouped under the general title of *Leiturgodia*, Friedrich Blume says, "No musician endeavored to deal with the sum total of all sections pertaining to the Latin Mass as systematically and comprehensively as did Michael Praetorius."[7] These works from 1607 and 1611 included: the *Musarum Sioniarum motectae et psalmi latini* (1607), Latin motets for four to 16 voices; the *Missodia Sionia* (1611), an entire collection of Mass settings, including both Ordinary and Proper texts; the *Hymnodia Sionia* (1611), 24 Latin hymns in 145 settings for two to eight voices, including six Latin organ hymns; the *Eulogodia Sionia* (1611), which contained settings of the Benedictus and the Deo dicamus ordered according to the church year and settings of the Benedicamus Domino from the works of Thomas Mancinus, Praetorius' predecessor at Wolfenbuettel; and the *Megalynodia Sionia* (1611), which contained 14 settings of the Magnificat, of which 11 are parodies of motets, madrigals, and chansons and three settings are apparently original compositions. Of particular interest are the first two Magnificat settings, which interpolate familiar German Christmas carols—apparently to be sung by the congregation—into the settings of the Latin Magnificat; the third setting interpolates Easter carols in a similar fashion.[8] Representative of these settings

---

[7] Friedrich Blume, *Protestant Church Music: A History* (New York: W. W. Norton & Co., 1974), 173.

[8] The practice of interpolating vernacular chorales into the Latin Magnificat apparently began in the late 1500s and persisted—despite some official attempts to repress it—at least until the time of Johann Sebastian Bach, who followed this practice in his early version of the Magnificat (in E flat) into which he interpolates the Christmas chorale "Vom Himmel hoch da komm ich her."

from the Latin liturgical works is the "Kyrie Paschale" (Ex. 25) from the *Missodia Sionia* (1611). It is clear from these works of Praetorius—as well as those of his predecessors—that the need for settings of the liturgical texts in Latin continued throughout the 16th century.

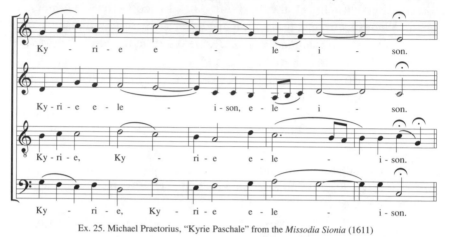

Ex. 25. Michael Praetorius, "Kyrie Paschale" from the *Missodia Sionia* (1611)

Included in the *Musae Sioniae Part VII* (1609) and the *Hymnodia Sionia* (1611) are Praetorius' few but highly significant works for organ. From 1609 are four large-scale compositions based on the Lutheran chorales "Ein feste Burg ist unser Gott," "Christ, unser Herr," "Wir glauben all," and a set of two variations on "Nun lob, mein Seel." These works are chorale motets for organ of gigantic proportions. The general texture of these organ works is typified in Ex. 26, a portion of the work on "Ein feste Burg ist unser Gott." From 1611 are six Latin hymn settings in the traditional *cantus-planus* style of Schlick and Cabezon with the melody in long notes in the bass part. Of these compositions Willi Apel says, "It is impossible to do justice to these monumental compositions. . . . They are the works of a master who, more than anybody else in this field, succeeded in combining the great achievements of the 16th century with

Ex. 26. Michael Praetorius, "Ein feste Burg ist unser Gott" for organ from *Musae Sioniae Part VII* (1609)

the novel ideas of the early 17th century."[9] Ex. 27 shows the beginning of Praetorius' setting for organ of the Latin hymn for Christmas "A solis ortus cardine." Through his work as an organ consultant, Praetorius learned much about the German organ of his day, which he described in painstaking detail in his *Syntagma musicum* (vol. II, 1619).[10] Worthy of note is Praetorius' collaboration with Esaias Compenius, the most famous organ builder of his day, with whom he co-authored a manuscript on the inspection of organs, the *Kurtzer Bericht wasz bey ueberliefferung einer Klein und grosverfertigten Orgell zu observiren.*[11]

Ex. 27. Michael Praetorius, "A solis ortus cardine" for organ from *Hymnodia Sionia* (1611)

While the center of Praetorius' musical activity was the chorale, its preservation and its continuation, these years also saw the appearance of Praetorius' only secular collection, *Terpsichore* (1612), a collection of more than 300 dances for instrumental ensemble in four to six parts. This was the fifth part—the only one completed—of a larger project, the *Musae aoniae*, which Praetorius envisioned as a secular counterpart to the *Musae Sioniae*. This collection contained settings of French dance melodies—apparently from the repertoire of French musicians at the court of Henry IV—that Praetorius had learned from Antoine Emeraud, one of two French dancing masters at the Wolfenbuettel court. The other, Pierre Francisque Caroubel, worked with Praetorius on the collection, contributing no fewer than 78 settings, most of which Praetorius carefully identified. The collection groups the individual movements into sets of the same dance type: all the *courantes* together, the *branles* together, etc. Ex. 28 is typical of these dance movements. While specific instruments are not

---

[9] Willi Apel, "Solo Instrumental Music," in *The Age of Humanism 1540–1630* (ed. Gerald Abraham; vol. IV of *The New Oxford History of Music;* London: Oxford University Press, 1968), 665.

[10] See also Paul Bunjes, *The Praetorius Organ* (St. Louis: Concordia, 1966).

[11] This work is often referred to as the *Orgeln Verdingnis* as Praetorius himself does in his *De organographia* in the *Syntagma musicum*, vols. II and III. See *Orgeln Verdingnis* (ed. Friedrich Blume; vol. 4 of *Kieler Beitraege zur Musikwissenschaft;* Wolfenbuettel and Berlin, 1936).

indicated, in the foreword to the collection, Praetorius speaks of the use of wind and brass instruments and even the use of organ and lute in the performance of these dances. The collection is characterized by David Munrow as ". . . no dry academic catalogue of dance species, but a deluxe edition of the best material for dance bands to choose from."[12]

Ex. 28. Michael Praetorius, instrumental dance movement from *Terpsichore* (1612)

Urania (1613), which appeared in the same year as Heinrich Julius' death, contained polychoral settings of chorales for two to four choirs and included instructions for placing the choirs in various parts of the church. These works are essentially homophonic and are influenced, as Praetorius himself says in his preface, by the "splendid composer and organist, Giovanni Gabrieli." Of particular interest are the instructions and suggestions in the introduction to *Urania* which reflect Praetorius' practical bent in arranging voices and instruments for more than one choir.

> One may also divide the four-part psalms among four choirs placed in different parts of the church when the variety provided by various kinds of instruments and the number of singers and instrumentalists is available. The music may be divided according to the following plan: Choir I—cantors or vocalists; Choir II—wind instruments such as trumpets and trombones; Choir III—recorders and flutes, the bass part, however, played by a bassoon, or in place of these, krummhorns and other similar instruments, or where such instruments are not available, four vocalists; Choir IV—stringed instruments, violins and cellos, accompanied by a lute, clavicembalo, harp, or theorbo (a deep lute) when one is available, or lacking all these a portativ organ or regal may be used. For each choir there should be at least one singer who has a fine, pure voice who should sing the hymn in the soprano, alto, or tenor part, so that the text may really be heard and understood by each person.

---

[12] David Munrow, from the album notes to *Music of Michael Praetorius*, Angel S-37091.

This quotation reflects several ideas worth noting: the various choirs are placed in different parts of the church; the term "choir" may mean voices, instruments, or a combination of both; the instrumental "choir" is made up of similar instruments; each "choir" must have at least one vocalist who sings the text; and the flexibility which allows for various substitutions when one or another instrument may not be available. Such a possible deployment of voices and instruments is visually depicted in a detailed woodcut which appears as part of the title page in a number of Praetorius' works.

The Later Years

Following the death of Duke Heinrich Julius in 1613 and a subsequent change of residence to Dresden until 1616, Praetorius began a period in which he traveled widely, serving for brief periods in places where he was called on to conduct, such as Naumberg (1614); Dresden (1614); Halle (1616); Magdeburg (1617/18)—where he worked with Samuel Scheidt and Heinrich Schuetz; Leipzig (1619); Nuremberg (1619); and Bayreuth (1619) (working again with Scheidt and Schuetz).

Fig. 8. Michael Praetorius with Thomas Mancinus and Esaias Korner in the funeral procession of Duke Heinrich Julius (1613)

In his later years, Praetorius conceived a large-scale plan titled *Polyhymnia ecclesiastica*, which would encompass the entire domain of church music in concerted style. Only three volumes of this projected 15-volume collection were completed. The first volume appeared in 1619 as the *Polyhymnia caduceatrix et panegyrica*. It contained large-scale works with independent instrumental accompaniment in the resplendent Venetian style, including two German Masses and a Magnificat in concertato style. The second volume was the *Polyhymnia exercitatrix* (1620), which contained Alleluias and German hymns for the school choirs in which the virtuosity of the Italian style of singing was clothed in settings for the evangelical chorales. In the introduction to this volume, Praetorius describes his purpose and method:

The Hallelujahs and German songs in this *Polyhymnia Exercitatrix* I originally arranged in order to lead and accustom my choirboys to practice and to develop their inclination and skill for singing. Now in order that other boys might likewise develop a similar inclination and love for such a skill and not let themselves be deterred and frightened off at the very outset by the many eighth and sixteenth notes, I have also arranged a simple form of the melody at places that might be too difficult.[13]

The setting of "Exultate, jubilate" is for two voices (sopranos or tenors) with *continuo* and four optional additional parts, any of which might be played on lower brass instruments or sung as the resources might be available. The final three measures (Ex. 29) illustrate Praetorius' provision of a simpler form (designated here with an asterisk) of the more elaborate melody when that might prove too difficult for the boys.

The third volume was the *Puercinium* (1621), a collection of 14 works to teach the Italian virtuoso style to choirboys. This collection used boy choirs, adult choirs, and instrumental accompaniment in magnificent large-scale works that reflected Praetorius' transition to the new Italian style. These massive chorale settings are, in a sense, Praetorius' answer to the late motets of Gabrieli. They reflect his use of the most novel features of the new Italian style and are the result of his periods of travel, during which he was able to direct huge gatherings of musicians. They reflect

Ex. 29. Michael Praetorius, "Exultate, jubilate" from *Polyhymnia exercitatrix* (1620)

---

[13] From the introduction to the *Polyhymnia exercitatrix* (1620), trans. by Carl Schalk.

especially his emphasis on spacing of musical forces, sonority, and a solemn pomp, rather than musical style.

Special mention must be made of Praetorius' *Syntagma musicum*, a musicological work of great significance published between 1614 and 1620. Projected as a four-volume work, only three volumes were completed: Volume I (1615), written in Latin, discusses the origins, history, and principles of sacred music—surprising in its breadth and scope because Praetorius never left his native Germany; Volume II (1619), written in German, is the *De organographia* and includes the *Theatrum instrumentorum* (1620), which gives a detailed account of musical instruments and their function, including a valuable series of illustrations drawn to

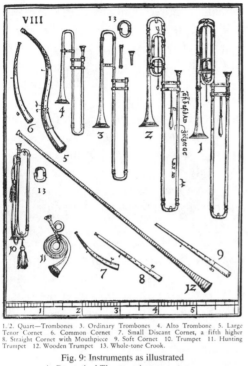

1. 2. Quart—Trombones 3. Ordinary Trombones 4. Alto Trombone 5. Large Tenor Cornet 6. Common Cornet 7. Small Discant Cornet, a fifth higher 8. Straight Cornet with Mouthpiece 9. Soft Cornet 10. Trumpet 11. Hunting Trumpet 12. Wooden Trumpet 13. Whole-tone Crook.

Fig. 9: Instruments as illustrated in Praetorius' *Theatrum instrumentorum*

scale; and Volume III, the *Termini musici* (1619), also written in German, which deals with notation, various forms of secular music of the early 17th century, methods of performance, and principles of choir training. The *Syntagma musicum* is one of the most important sources of information concerning the music of the late 16th and early 17th centuries.

Praetorius subsequently returned to Wolfenbuettel where he died on February 15, 1621, at the age of 50. As he awaited death, Praetorius wrote a setting of Psalm 116 for Bernard Groszmann's famous collection *Angst der Hoellen* (1623), published two years after Praetorius' death. Praetorius bequeathed the greater part of a not inconsiderable fortune for the care of the poor.

Michael Praetorius was one of the most prolific and versatile composers of his time. Once considered by some a pedant, today Praetorius is viewed as one of the most influential and significant personalities in the history of Lutheran church music. A summary of his work reveals the thoroughness with which he approached the task of providing music for the church of his day.

Like Hans Leo Hassler, Praetorius' career was built largely on the musical tradition of di Lasso. His concern for the chorale—in search of which he diligently and systematically scoured many parts of Germany— and its preservation in a variety of kinds of music has earned him the title "conservator of the chorale." In this sense he was, as Blume remarked, "literally the successor of Johann Walter" and "the most vigorous representative of Lutheran orthodoxy in the whole history of church music."[14] In his *Musae Sioniae,* Praetorius codified the various types of vocal treatment of the chorale. In his Latin liturgical works, he presented a series of collections that attest to the continuing importance of the Latin language in the worship of Lutherans into the 17th century. And in his *Polyhymnia* collections—though he never saw Italy—Praetorius reflects the growing importance of the Italian musical innovations, with the single exception of monody, which would have an increasing influence on Lutheran music in the years to come.

Praetorius is the prime example of the Lutheran composers between Luther and Bach who could be open to the new musical developments of his time without breaking ties to the old. It was, in fact, the older tradition which for Praetorius and others who followed him provided the musical material—the chorale—on the basis of which the newer styles would be incorporated into the song of the church. In this way Praetorius, as with others of his day, avoided the temptation to isolate his art from the new developments in Europe—developments which would ultimately result in a profound division of music between the *style antico* and the *style moderno*. In what at first may seem a strange juxtaposition of concerns—for perpetuating the chorale, for providing a large repertoire of music for the Latin Mass, and for a simultaneous concern for developing the use of all the newer musical devices of his time—Praetorius' life, career, and, above all, his music help to explain why and how Lutheran music of the 17th century held so firmly and for so long to its roots in the tradition, progressively rejuvenating it and adapting it to the changing styles of the times.

---

[14] Blume, op. cit., 159.

MICHAEL PRAETORIUS

| 1570 | 1580 | 1590 | 1600 | 1610 | 1620 | 1630 |

Musae Sioniae (1605–10)

Leiturgodia (1607, 1611)
Motectae et psalmi latini
Missodia Sionia
Hymnodia Sionia
Eulogodia Sionia
Megalynodia Sionia

Musae aoniae (1612)
Terpsichore

Urania (1613)

Polyhymnia ecclesiastica (1619–21)
Polyhymnia caduceatrix
Polyhymnia exercitatrix
Puercinium

Guide to Michael Praetorius' Collected Works

Praetorius, Michael. *Gesamtausgabe der musikalische Werke* (*GmW*). Edited by Friedrich Blume. 21 vols. Wolfenbuettel: Moeseler Verlag, 1928–60.

1605–10	*Musae Sioniae* (Parts I–IX)

Part I (1605) and Parts II–IV (1607) (*GmW* 1, 2, 3, 4) contain 116 pieces for two and three choirs, including a German Te Deum. Polyphonic and polychoral motets reflect the influence of Lassus.

Part V (1607) (*GmW* 5) contains 166 pieces for two to eight voices.

Part VI (1609) (GmW 6) contains 200 settings, mostly in four-part cantional style, for the major festivals of the church year.

Part VII (1609) (*GmW* 7) contains 244 settings of Catechism, Communion, and other chorales in cantional style. Included are the three German organ hymns ("Ein feste Burg ist unser Gott," "Christ, unser Herr," and "Wir glauben all"), and a set of variations on "Nun lob, mein Seel."

Part VIII (1610) (*GmW* 8) contains 322 four-part cantional settings of morning and evening hymns, songs for the table, songs of the church, for death and burial, etc.

Part IX (1610) (*GmW* 9) contains 216 settings for two and three voices (a few for four and five voices).

The *Musae Sioniae* contains a total of 1,244 settings ranging from simple cantional settings to through-composed chorale motets with and without *cantus firmus*. It is a compendium of the history of the treatment of the chorale melody of its time, illustrating the possibilities of choir, soloists, vocal and instrumental settings, but without *basso continuo*.

1607	*Musarum Sioniarum motectae et psalmi latini* (*GmW* 10)

Fifty-two Latin motets for four to 16 voices (one to four choirs) with clearly indicated solo passages; other sections indicated for voices and instruments together. Includes some compositions of Porta, Palestrina, and others.

1611   *Missodia Sionia (GmW* 11)
A collection of settings of Latin texts for the Mass. Kyries
and Glorias noted as in *contrapuncto simplici* or *contrapunc-
to colorato.* Contains sections entitled *Mystochordia*
(Versicles, Collects), *Symbolodia* (two Credo settings),
Heirodipnodia (Prefaces, Sanctus, Benedictus, Agnus Dei,
Subcommunion, Amens, 10 Glorias, Introit settings), and an
eight-voice Mass ordinary.

Hymnodia Sionia (GmW 12)
Twenty-four Latin hymns for the church year in 145 settings for two to eight voices. Includes several Latin organ
hymns.

Eulogodia Sionia (GmW 13)
Sixty settings of the Benedicamus and Deo dicamus
ordered according to the church year. Includes 12 settings of
the Benedicamus Domino from the works of Thomas
Mancinus, Praetorius' predecessor in Wolfenbuettel.

Megalynodia Sionia (GmW 14)
Fourteen settings of the Magnificat that parody motets,
madrigals, and chansons and several original settings, some
of which intersperse popular German and Latin songs
between the verses of the canticle.

1612   *Terpsichore (GmW* 15)
Four- to six-part settings of French dance melodies for use
at the Wolfenbuettel court; instrumentation not specified.

1613   *Urania (GmW* 16)
Polychoral settings of 28 chorales for two, three, and four
choirs, including directions for placing the choirs in the various parts of the church and for the use of instruments with
these settings.

1619   *Polyhymnia caduceatrix et panegyrica (GmW* 17)
Thirty-nine large-scale choral works with independent
instrumental accompaniment with *basso continuo.* Example
of the "resplendent Venetian style." Contains two German
Masses that employ chorale tunes and a German Magnificat
in concertato style.

1620   *Polyhymnia exercitatrix (GmW* 18)

Eight settings of short psalm texts with Hallelujah and six settings of chorales, all for two to four voices with three to four instruments in concertato style.

1621   *Puercinium (GmW* 19)

Collection of 14 large-scale works for four-part boys' choir with three- to four-part adult choir (usually ATTB), instruments, and *continuo.* Written to teach choirboys the Italian style with the material of the German chorale.

———

Miscellaneous Works (GmW 20)

Includes two Litany settings, four Latin motets, three chorale settings, a setting of Psalm 116, and several other pieces.

General Index to the Complete Musical Works (GmW 21)

Selected References for Further Reading

Primary Sources:

Praetorius, Michael. *Gesamtausgabe der musikalische Werke.* Edited by Friedrich Blume. 21 vols. Wolfenbuettel: Moeseler Verlag, 1928–60.

Praetorius, Michael. *Syntagma musicum.* Facsimile edition edited by Wilibald Gurlitt. 3 vols. Kassel: Baerenreiter, 1958–59.

Secondary Sources:

Blankenburg, Walter. "Praetorius, Michael." Pages 188–92 in vol. 15 of *The New Grove Dictionary of Music and Musicians.* Edited by Stanley Sadie. New York: Macmillan, 1980.

Bunjes, Paul. *The Praetorius Organ.* St. Louis: Concordia, 1966.

Buszin, Walter E. "Lutheran Church Music in the Age of Classical Lutheran Theology: Hans Leo Hassler and Michael Praetorius." Pages 62–76 in vol. 1 of *The Symposium on 17th Century Lutheranism.* Edited by A. C. Piepkorn, Robert Preus, and Erwin Luecker. St. Louis: Concordia, 1962.

Forchert, Arno. "Praetorius, Michael." Cols. 1560–72 in vol. 10 of *Die Musik in Geschichte und Gegenwart.* Kassel u. Basel: Baerenreiter, 1962.

Gurlitt, Wilibald. *Michael Praetorius (Creuzburgensis) Sein Leben und seine Werke.* Hildesheim: Georg Olms Verlag, 1968.

Messerli, Carlos. "Michael Praetorius, Polychoral Music, and the Fifty Days of Easter." *Church Music* 73.1 (1973): 17–27.

Riedel, Johannes. "Vocal Leisen Settings in the Baroque Era." Pages 95–109 in vol. 5 of *The Musical Heritage of the Church*. Edited by Theodore Hoelty-Nickel. St. Louis: Concordia, 1959.

Samuel, Harold. "Michael Praetorius on Concertato Style." Pages 95–109 in *Cantors at the Crossroads: Essays on Church Music in Honor of Walter E. Buszin*. Edited by Johannes Riedel. St. Louis: Concordia, 1967.

Spiess, Lincoln. "Michael Praetorius Creuzburgensis: Church Musician and Scholar." Pages 68–77 in vol. 5 of *The Musical Heritage of the Church*. Edited by Theodore Hoelty-Nickel. St. Louis: Concordia, 1959.

6

Johann Hermann Schein

Cantor of St. Thomas, Leipzig

Fig. 10. Johann Hermann Schein

Within the span of three short years—between 1585 and 1587—three men were born who were to significantly affect the course of Lutheran church music. In contrast to Johann Walter, for example, whose roots were firmly established in the musical practice of the late Renaissance, these three men—Johann Hermann Schein, Samuel Scheidt, and Heinrich Schuetz—were to bring the music of Lutheran worship in touch with the new musical developments of their day in a way that had not been true before. None of these three men abandoned the earlier heritage; in fact each wrote significant music in the so-called "old style," and all upheld the necessity for young composers to be thoroughly acquainted with and trained in the craft of composition according to the received practice. It was never a matter of abandoning and moving beyond the old, but it was receiving the heritage and building on to it as the music of the church moved into the future.

In contrast to both Hans Leo Hassler and Michael Praetorius, whose efforts reflected the beginnings of the transition from the Renaissance to the Baroque in Germany, Johann Hermann Schein stands out as one of the greatest among the generation of German composers slightly younger than Praetorius who brought the new Italian style to its first peak of greatness on German soil. Of all the composers considered here, Schein's life was the shortest; he lived only to the age of 44. Yet the impact of this illustrious predecessor of Johann Sebastian Bach in Leipzig was significant. Schein's contribution was both musical and literary, his literary skills reflected in the large number of his texts which he set to music.[1]

---

[1] Schein's original text "Mach's mit mir Gott" set to his original tune—also "Mach's mit mir Gott"—is still found in current German Lutheran hymnals (for example, the *Evangelisches Kirchengesangbuch fuer selbstaendige Evangelisch-Lutherische Kirche*, 1992, Nr. 321). Schein's tune—first published in broadsheet (1628) and later included in his *Cantional* (1645)—is based on a melody of Bartholomaeus Gesius of 1605.

The Early Years

Johann Hermann Schein was born on January 20, 1586, in Gruenhaim near Annaberg in Saxony, the fifth child of Hieronymus and Judith Schein (nee Schacht). Hieronymus was a Lutheran pastor, a devout adherent of the Lutheran Confessions, having entered the ministry later in life at the urging of Polycarp Leiser the Elder. After the death of Hieronymus in 1593, the family moved to Dresden. In 1599 the 13-year-old Johann Hermann became a soprano choirboy at the court chapel, where he came under the tutelage of Rogier Michael, director of chapel music, and Andreas Petermann.

Following a brief matriculation at the University of Leipzig, Schein was admitted to the electoral school at Schulpforta on May 18, 1603, a school that specialized in music and the humanities. After studying at the school at Pforta until 1607—where his teachers were Bartholomaeus Scheraeus and Martin Rothe, and where it is likely that he came under the influence of Erhard Bodenschatz, cantor at Schulpforta (1600-03) and later editor of the important collection *Florilegium Portense* (1603/18)— Schein went to the University of Leipzig early in 1608, where he remained until 1612 studying law. At that time the cantor at the *Thomaskirche* was Seth Calvisius, the predecessor of Erhard Bodenschatz at Schulpforta.

During his time in Leipzig, Schein produced his first musical work, the *Venuskraenzlein oder neue Weltliche Lieder* (1609), a secular collection— similar in form and content to works by Gastoldi and Hassler—containing 16 five-voice songs and one eight-voice song, the voice parts proceeding generally in similar rhythm (Ex. 30). In addition this collection contained several instrumental *gagliarda,* intradas, and canzona.[2] What one sees

Fig. 11. Students gathered for music-making in Leipzig (ca. 1625)

---

[2] Three of Schein's poems for this collection are acrostics on the name of Sidonia Hoesel, most likely a childhood sweetheart, whom he later married in 1616.

here is the monodic principle being adapted to polyphony. Written for the bicentenary of Leipzig University and printed in Wittenberg,

Ex. 30. Johann Hermann Schein, "Ringstum mich schwebet Traurigkeit" from *Venuskraenzlein* (1609)

it was dedicated to Wolfgang Lebzelter. Figure 11 shows a typical group of students gathered for music-making about 1625 in Leipzig. It was for just such groups that this collection and such later collections as Schein's *Studentenschmaus* were written.

At Weissenfels and Weimar (1613–16)

In 1613, at the instigation of Gottfried von Wolffersdorff, a fellow pupil with Schein at the school at Pforta, the 27-year-old Schein became teacher and *Hausmusik Director* in Wolffersdorff's household at Weissenfels. Two years later, on May 21, 1615, Schein became the *Hofkapellmeister* for Duke Johann Ernst in Weimar, having been recommended for this position by his friend Wolffersdorff.

In 1615 Schein's first collection of sacred works appeared, the *Cymbalum Sionium*, a collection of 30 quasi-Venetian motets on German and Latin texts—Responses, proses, psalms, Gospels—for five to 12 voices (Ex. 31). This collection belongs to the *prima prattica* in which Schein takes as his model such composers as Calvisius, Hassler, Lechner, Praetorius, and others in the polyphonic motet style of Orlando di Lasso. Despite their generally retrospective character, these motets nevertheless indicate a developing personal style through such means as the development of a clearer formal structure, the adoption of concertato techniques, the beginnings of a clearer use of greater contrast and dramatic tech-

niques, and in the careful attention to bringing the textual content closer
to the listener through more adequate musical forms.

Ex. 31. Johann Hermann Schein, "Verbum caro factum est" from *Cymbalum Sionium* (1615)

Cantor at St. Thomas, Leipzig (1616–30)

On August 19, 1616, Schein auditioned for the position of cantor at St.
Thomas, Leipzig—a position that had been vacant since the death of Seth
Calvisius the preceding November. Schein began his work there in late
September or early October and became an illustrious predecessor of such
future *Thomaskantors* as Johann Schelle, Johann Kuhnau, and Bach.
Schein retained this position until his death in 1630. As was common for
many in similar positions, Schein—in addition to his musical responsibilities at the *Thomaskirche* and the *Nicolaikirche*—was required to teach 14
hours a week in the school—10 hours of Latin and four hours of singing—
a situation of his employment about which he complained because he
wished to devote more time to his musical composition. Schein married
Sidonia Hoesel[3] on February 12, 1616, a union which was blessed with
three daughters (Susanna, Susanna Sidonia, and Johanna Judith) who died
in infancy and two sons (Johann Samuel and Johann Hermann). After only
eight years of marriage, Schein's wife died in 1624. The following year he
married Elisabeth von der Perre, a union which resulted in five children
(Johanna Elisabeth, Johanna Susanna, Johannes Zacharias, Hieronymus,
and Maria Salome), four of whom also died in early childhood.

---

[3] See preceding note.

The close connection between Schein and the people of Leipzig whom he served can be seen in the numerous wedding and funeral pieces which he wrote during the course of his career in Leipzig. Among Schein's intimate friends were Samuel Scheidt and Heinrich Schuetz. Among his pupils were Paul Flemming (who wrote a commemorative anagram to his former teacher), Christoph Schultze, Andreas Unger, Christian Knorr, Johannes Kegler, Marcus Dictericus, and Daniel Schade.

In addition to the devastation to his family life caused in part by the deprivations and diseases of the Thirty Years War, Schein himself suffered from poor health through much of his later life, being afflicted with tuberculosis, gout, scurvy, and kidney stones. He died in 1630 at the age of 44. Johann Hoepner, pastor of the Nicolai church, preached the funeral sermon. Heinrich Schuetz, who visited Schein on his deathbed, followed the wish of the dying Schein and wrote a six-part motet "Das ist je gewiszlich wahr" (based on 1 Timothy 1:15–17), which appeared in Dresden in 1631. Following Schein's death in 1630, Tobias Michael, son of Rogier Michael, was chosen to fill the vacant post at St. Thomas. Four years after Schein's death, Elisabeth married Hans Roesch of Nuremberg.

Among Schein's secular works from his years in Leipzig, his *Banchetto musicale* (1617) stands out as particularly important. This collection of 20 instrumental suites, dedicated to Duke Johann Ernst, stands in contrast to Praetorius' *Terpsichore,* which was music for actual dancing. Schein's collection shows the developing stylization, formal expansion, and heightened compositional sophistication which was transforming simple dance pieces into more richly expressive pieces of abstract music. In contrast to Praetorius' dance collection where all the examples of a particular dance type were grouped together, the music in the *Banchetto musicale* was grouped into suites, each suite containing *paduana, gagliarda, courante, allemande,* and *tripla.* Ex. 32 shows the beginning of an *allemande* from one of these suites. In addition, Schein frequently employed variations on the same basic melodic motive for each of the movements throughout a suite. In this collection, "the variation suite assumed its classic form";[4] and while intended for any variety of instruments, Schein suggests the priority of stringed instruments.

[4] Manfred F. Bukofzer, *Music in the Baroque Era* (New York: W. W. Norton & Co., 1947), 113.

Ex. 32. Johann Hermann Schein, "Allemande" from *Banchetto musicale* (1617)

Schein's other secular works included the *Musica boscareccia* or *Wald-Liederlein* (1621, 1626, 1628), a collection of 50 strophic songs for two sopranos and bass in which the bass part was identical with the *basso continuo*. These pieces were strophic, few-voiced concertatos with obligatory *basso continuo* with occasional slight *gorgia* passages (Ex. 33). Schein's indebtedness to the Italian style is reflected also in the Italian dynamic and tempo indications. Schein suggests a variety of performance possibilities—from *a cappella* singing to solo songs with *continuo* for either soprano or tenor—and leaves the choice of voice registers to the performers, as many other Italian composers had done before. Among his suggestions for performance, the option for performance by solo voice with *basso continuo* reflects Schein's appropriation of the monodic principle in this secular collection. This principle was also carried out in his sacred collections, particularly the *Opella nova* from these same years.

Ex. 33. Johann Hermann Schein, "O Sternenäugelein" from *Musica boscareccia* (1621)

The *Diletti pastorali, Hirtenlust* (1624) was a collection of 15 German *continuo* madrigals for five voices and instruments in through-composed form. These secular madrigals were more clearly designed for solo rather than choral performance (Ex. 34). This collection, where contrapuntal and chordal writing are mixed, is a kind of parallel to the sacred madrigals of the *Fontana d'Israel*. Schein's last collection of secular music was the

Ex. 34. Johann Hermann Schein, "O Amarilli" from *Diletti pastorali* (1624)

Studentenschmaus (1626), a collection of five-part drinking songs in which he returns to the simple choral song style of the earlier *Venuskraenzlein*. According to one authority, these works are "among the finest examples of student music in the last phase of the secular poly-phonic *Lied* of the baroque period."[5] "Holla, gut Gsell" (Ex. 35) is a representative example of this style.

Of Schein's sacred collections, the *Opella nova* (Part I, 1618; Part II, 1626) stands out as worthy of particular mention. Here in these few-voiced concertatos the Italian affective spirit manifests itself most clearly.[6] Subtitled *Geistliche Konzerte, mit 3. 4. und 5. Stimmen zusampt dem General-Bass, auff italianische Invention*, Schein in this collection attempted a highly subjective interpretation of the words of the chorale.[7] In the attempt to subject the chorale melodies to a more personal interpre-

Ex. 35. Johann Hermann Schein, "Holla, gut Gsell" from *Studentenschmaus* (1626)

---

[5] Kurt Gudewill, "German Secular Song," in *The Age of Humanism 1540–1630* (ed. Gerald Abraham; vol. IV of *The New Oxford History of Music*; London: Oxford University Press, 1968), 123.

[6] According to Bukofzer, the term *Geistliche Konzerte* appears here for the first time in German music. See Bukofzer, op. cit., 85.

[7] The figural music of the Lutheran church reflected two methods of interpretation of the "Word." While they had the concertato style in common, the first was bound by a chorale *cantus firmus*; the second was bound only by the subjective imagination of the composer. Schein's *Opella nova* belongs to this second approach.

Ex. 36. Johann Hermann Schein, "Nun komm, der Heiden Heiland" from *Opella nova I* (1618)

tation, he "distorted the chorale tunes, broke them up into fragments, viv-
ified the rhythm, and infused them with extraneous chromaticism or *gorgia*."[8] Part I, dedicated to Leipzig's mayor and town council, is (with only
one exception) based on chorale texts and tunes for the liturgical year for
one or two treble voices, the *cantus firmus* usually intact in another (usually male) voice, and *basso continuo*. Ex. 36, a setting of the Advent hymn
"Nun komm, der Heiden Heiland," illustrates Schein's procedure as well

---

[8] Bukofzer, op. cit., 85.

as his use of the *cantus firmus* set in a straightforward manner in the tenor
part. The one exception in Part I to the basing of settings on chorales is "O
Jesu Christe," a freely composed melody with violin *obbligato* (Ex. 37).
This foreshadows the general practice in Part II of the *Opella nova*.
Dedicated to Nuremberg's mayor and town council, Part II contains small
konzerte with *basso continuo*; solo concertos for tenor and bass with
obbligato instruments and *basso continuo*; and *konzerte* for one to three
soloists, choir, *obbligato* instruments, and *basso continuo*.[9] The *Opella
nova*, especially Part II, represents the most serious attempt thus far to
assimilate the Italian monodic principle into German music.

Ex. 37. Johann Hermann Schein, "O Jesu Christe" from *Opella nova I* (1618)

Schein's *Opella nova* clearly reflects two paths that lay before
Lutheran composers as they attempted to assimilate the new affective
approach. Part I, considered "a milestone in the development of the
chorale concertato,"[10] uses the texts and tunes of the traditional chorales.
Not content, however, with the simple "presentation" of the chorale as in
Praetorius, Schein attempts a highly subjective "interpretation" of the
chorale. Part II, however, moves away from the use of the chorale tune,
freely exercising the composer's musical imagination apart from any previously existing melodic material. Many composers pursued these two
courses which Schein set forth in his *Opella nova*, notably Samuel Scheidt
in his *Newe geistliche Conzerten*. Other later masters of the *chorale concertato* include: in the North German School—Thomas Selle, Matthias
Weckmann, and Franz Tunder; in the Central German School—Andreas
Hammerschmidt and the three Thomas cantors between Schein and

---

[9] In *Opella nova II,* the relation between chorale text and melody is almost completely
severed, as it is in the single example "O Jesu Christe" in *Opella nova I.*

[10] Bukofzer, op. cit., 85.

Kuhnau, Tobias Michael, Sebastian Knuepfer, and Johann Schelle; and in the South German School—Johann Staden and Erasmus Kindermann.

The *Fontana d'Israel* (1623), or *Israelsbruennlein,* reflects the blending of the madrigal style with that of the motet in which the influence of Monteverdi's madrigal settings is evident. It is the sacred counterpart to the *weltliche Madrigalen* of the *Diletti pastorali* (1624). This collection has 26 five-part madrigals with *continuo,* the texts taken from the Old Testament (23), Revelation (one), and two free texts, possibly by Schein himself. Included is the frequently sung "Die mit Traenen saen." The chromatic motif in this motet (Ex. 38) reflects a new expressiveness

Ex. 38. Johann Hermann Schein, "Die mit Traenen saen" from *Fontana d'Israel* (1623)

not seen before in quite this manner. "Was betruebst du dich, meine Seele" (Ex. 39) reflects more of the madrigal style in this collection.

Ex. 39. Johann Hermann Schein, "Was betruebst du dich, meine Seele" from *Fontana d'Israel* (1623)

The last of Schein's collections of sacred music is his *Cantional oder Gesangbuch Augspurgischer Confession* (1627). An enlarged edition appeared in 1645, some 15 years after Schein's death in 1630. The collection contained 286 hymns, most in simple four-part cantional style. The second edition enlarged the corpus by 27 additional settings. Typical of the simple four-part settings is the "Veni Redemptor gentium" (Ex. 40).

Ex. 40. Johann Hermann Schein, "Veni Redemptor gentium" from *Cantional* (1627)

Seven pieces in the *Cantional* have somewhat more involved contrapuntal settings in five parts attached to the simpler four-part setting, of which "Nun komm, der Heiden Heiland" (Ex. 41) is an example. The collection is particularly noteworthy because the bass part contains figures *fuer die Organisten, Instrumentisten und Lautenisten,* thus definitely establishing a formal organ *continuo* part, a practice which was already evident in the *Hamburg Melodien Gesangbuch* (1604). The organ accompaniment of the chorale, therefore, as reflected in Schein's *Cantional,* was an invention of the early Baroque period.

Ex. 41. Johann Hermann Schein, "Nun komm, der Heiden Heiland" from *Cantional* (1627)

Schein's *Cantional* replaced the *Harmonia cantionum ecclestiasticarum* (1597, 5th ed. 1622) of his predecessor Seth Calvisius. It portends the waning of the line of simple cantionals begun by Lucas Osiander in 1586. The preface was written by Polycarp Leiser, and in general the collection reflects the newer emphasis on somewhat more personal and subjective hymns. Many of these settings were taken over into later collections, but few of Schein's settings have remained in use to the present. Among those songs with texts and music by Schein himself—he composed new tunes for 57 of the hymns, for 43 he wrote his own words—might be noted a Ten Commandments hymn, 22 "meditations" on psalms, and 18 songs on the topic of death. These latter songs may well reflect the fact that many of Schein's children and his first wife died as a result of the pestilence brought on by the Thirty Years War.

While it is true that Schein's secular works are somewhat more numerous than his religious works, his sacred compositions have an importance all their own. The significance of the earlier tradition for Schein's music reflects itself most clearly in his *Cymbalum Sionium* (1615) and in the *Cantional*, where the use of the figured bass, however, reflects the direction such collections would take in the years ahead. But it is especially in his *Opella nova* (1618/26) and his *Fontana d'Israel* (1623), among Schein's sacred works, that the Italian madrigal and the growing importance of monody for German music make their greatest contribution. With Schein the expressive devices of the Italian Baroque are absorbed into German music in a way not seen or heard before. The sensitivity with which Schein sought to interpret the words in his music reflects a concern for a "biblical exegesis" which would find its greatest expression in the 17th century in the work of Heinrich Schuetz, who at the time of Schein's death had just reached the midpoint in his life and career.

JOHANN HERMANN SCHEIN

1580	1590	1600	1610	1620	1630	1640

Venuskraenzlein (1609)

Cymbalum Sionium (1615)

Banchetto musicale (1617)

Opella nova (1618/26)

Musica boscareccia (1621/26/28)

Fontana d'Israel (1623)

Diletti pastorali (1624)

Studentenschmaus (1626)

Cantional oder Gesangbuch Augspurgischer Confession (1627/45)

Guide to Johann Hermann Schein's Collected Works

Schein, Johann Hermann. *Neue Ausgabe saemlicher Werke* (*NA*). Edited
by Adam Adrio. Currently 8 vols. Kassel u. Basel: Baerenreiter
Verlag, 1963—. (In progress).[11]

1609   *Venuskraenzlein oder neue Weltliche Lieder* (*NA* 6)
            Edited by Marianne and Siegmund Helms. Seventeen sec-
            ular songs for five and eight voices plus eight instrumental
            intradas, *gagliarda*, and canzona in five and six parts.

1615   *Cymbalum Sionium* (*NA* 3)
            Edited by Arno Forchert and Claudia Theis. Thirty motets
            for five to 12 voices with both Latin and German texts.

1617   *Banchetto musicale* (*NA* 9)
            Edited by Dieter Krickeberg. Twenty instrumental suites
            for five voices. *Paduana, gagliarda, courante, allemande,
            and tripla.*

1618/26   *Opella nova, Geistliche Konzerte, mit 3. 4. und 5.
            Stimmen zusampt dem General-Bass, auff italianische
            Invention* (*NA* 4, 5)
            Edited by Walter Werbeck. Part I (1618) contains 30 set-
            tings: 29 based on chorales set for two or three voices with
            figured bass and an occasional *obbligato* instrument and one
            free piece for solo voice with *obbligato* instrument and fig-
            ured bass. This collection contains the first German examples
            of the small concertato form for two or three voices with fig-
            ured bass.
                Part II (1626) contains 32 settings (five with Latin texts, 27
            with German texts) for three, four, five, and six voices with
            figured bass. Eight are based on chorale tunes, the great
            majority being free pieces.

---

[11] Arthur Pruefer, ed., *Johann Hermann Scheins Saemtliche Werke* (7 vols.; Leipzig:
Breitkopf u. Haertel, 1903–23) is an earlier and less complete edition, containing only
the *Venuskraenzlein, Banchetto musicale, Musica boscareccia, Diletti pastorali,
Cymbalum Sionium*, and *Opella nova.*

1621/26/28 *Musica boscareccia (Wald-Liederlein), Villanellen zu 3*
          Stimmen mit General-Bass (NA 7)
             Edited by Joachim Thalmann. Part I (*Erster Teil,* 1621) has
          16 compositions in three parts (SSB) with *continuo.*
             Part II (*Ander Teil,* 1626) has 16 compositions in three
          parts (SSB) with *basso continuo.*
             Part III (*Dritter Teil,* 1628) has 18 compositions in three
          parts (SSB) with *basso continuo.*

1623   *Fontana d'Israel (Israelsbruennlein) (NA 1)*
             Edited by Adam Adrio. Twenty-six spiritual madrigals after
          the Italian model, 25 for five voices (SSATB) with general-
          bass, one for six voices (SSATTB).

1624   *Diletti pastorali, Hirtenlust (NA 8)*
             Edited by Adam Adrio. Fifteen secular madrigals for five
          voices and figured bass.

1626   *Studentenschmaus (NA 6)*
             Edited by Marianne and Siegmund Helms. Five secular
          songs for five voices with figured bass.

1627/45   *Cantional oder Gesangbuch Augspurgischer Confession*
          (NA 2)
             Edited by Adam Adrio. The first edition contained 286 set-
          tings to which Schein's successor, Tobias Michael, added 27
          in 1645. Of the 313 songs in the second edition, four are sim-
          ple unison melodies, 200 are for four voices, 27 are for five
          voices, one is for six voices (by Seth Calvisius). In addition
          there are seven more contrapuntal settings alongside the sim-
          ple homophonic settings that constitute the bulk of the set-
          tings. The remaining songs contain only the text without
          music. The appearance of figures with the bass vocal part
          indicates the beginning of a new development in the history
          of the cantionals, which ultimately becomes the history of the
          choralbuch.

Selected References for Further Reading

Primary Source:

Schein, Johann Hermann. *Neue Ausgabe saemlicher Werke*. Edited by
    Adam Adrio. Currently 8 vols. Kassel u. Basel: Baerenreiter Verlag,
    1963—. (In progress).

Secondary Sources:

Adrio, Adam. "Schein, Johann Hermann." Cols. 1642–54 in vol. 11 of
    Die Musik in Geschichte und Gegenwart. Kassel u. Basel:
    Baerenreiter Verlag, 1963.

Snyder, Kerala Johnson. "Schein, Johann Hermann." Pages 612–19 in
    vol. 16 of *The New Grove Dictionary of Music and Musicians*.
    Edited by Stanley Sadie. New York: Macmillan, 1980.

7

Samuel Scheidt

Musician of Halle

Without a doubt, the musical contributions of Samuel Scheidt are most prominently associated with his liturgical organ compositions for the Lutheran service—represented by his *Tabulatura nova* (1624) and the *Tabulaturbuch, 100 geistliche Lieder und Psalmen* (1650). Equally significant in connection with his organ music is his adoption and use of the "new tablature," replacing the old German tablature in which letters, numbers, or other signs are used to indicate the notes and rhythm. But these significant contributions should not overshadow Scheidt's large output of choral music and settings for few-voiced ensembles. His *Cantiones sacrae* (1620) in the older polychoral style is worthy to be compared with similar works of Praetorius; and his *Newe geistliche Conzerten* (1631ff) are significant works in the developing few-voiced concertato style. These works, among others, deserve a greater hearing and revival in performance as one attempts to assess the contributions of this most important composer of the early Baroque.

Samuel Scheidt was born early in November in the year 1587 (he was baptized November 4, 1587), the oldest son of Konrad Scheidt and Anna Achtmann. Born in the city of Halle, he would be associated with the city throughout his entire professional life. And on Good Friday, March 24, 1654, Scheidt died in the city of his birth.

The city of Halle at the close of the 16th century was a leading cultural and commercial center. The court life, its churches, and its schools all helped to attract to the city artists, poets, and people of learning. The city maintained international contacts, and merchants came from Scotland, goldsmiths from Switzerland, painters and woodcarvers from the Netherlands, and musicians from England and Italy. It was into such an environment that Scheidt was born, grew up, and eventually spent his entire adult life and career as a musician.

The families of both of Scheidt's parents—the Scheidts and the Achtmanns—were on intimate terms and associated with a variety of people of various artistic leanings. Among them were the Compenius family, which achieved fame in the world of organ building, the organists Wolff Eisentraut and Salomon Kramer, and the Stellwagen family, famous for woodcarving. Two younger sons in the Scheidt family also became musicians of note: Gottfried (1593–1661)—who like Samuel studied with

Sweelinck and was later court organist in Altenburg—and Christian (1600–after 1628), who served as organist in Eisleben, Alsleben, and Frankenhausen. Samuel Scheidt was also the only musician of the seven discussed here whose father was a barkeep and who eventually became a *Ratsbierschenck*—a municipal beer and wine steward.

Very little is known of Samuel's early life, but it is likely that he, like his brother Gottfried, attended the Lutheran Gymnasium in his early years where he came under the musical influence of the Cantor Matthaeus Birkner and his successor, Georg Schetz. Already in about 1603/4, at the

Fig. 12. Samuel Scheidt

young age of 17, Scheidt served as organist at the *Moritzkirche*, the youngest of the three churches of Halle, the others being the *St. Marienkirche* and *St. Ulrich*.

Scheidt remained at the *Moritzkirche* for about three years, at which time—about 1607 or 1608—he left Halle to go to Amsterdam where he studied for two years with Jan Pieterszoon Sweelinck (1562–1621), the prominent Dutch organist and composer. Sweelinck had adopted much of the style of the contemporary English keyboard composers—most notably John Bull (1563–1628)—and had, in Manfred Bukofzer's opinion, "amalgamated in his music the modern Venetian forms with the figurative techniques of the English virginal-ists."[1] The use of these figurative techniques, together with the use of chromaticism (from *chroma* or *color*) so common among these English composers can be seen in much of Scheidt's music. This period of study with Sweelinck was an important formative influence on the young Scheidt, who carried these ideas back to Germany and integrated them into his developing keyboard idiom. From this period there is extant an interesting series of eight variations on a Spanish *paduana* in which four movements were written by Sweelinck and four by Scheidt.[2] These four

---

[1] Manfred F. Bukofzer, *Music in the Baroque Era* (New York: W. W. Norton & Co., 1947), 74.

[2] See Samuel Scheidt, *Werke,* vol. 5 (eds. Gottlieb Harms and Christhard Mahrenholz; Ugrino Verlag, 1923). Hereafter *SW*. For four of these variations, see also Hertha Schweiger, *A Brief Compendium of Early Organ Music* (New York: G. Schirmer, Inc., 1943).

variations by Scheidt (Ex. 42) show his early attempts to explore the various possibilities in combining a *cantus firmus* with a variety of rhythmic patterns. This idea would be carried out with much greater thoroughness in his *Tabulatura nova* (1624).

Ex. 42. Samuel Scheidt, four variations on a Spanish *paduana* (c. 1609)

In 1609 Scheidt returned to Halle where he became court organist for Margrave Christian Wilhelm of Brandenburg, in which capacity he played for the morning and evening services at the Magdalene Chapel and also served as musician for social functions at the court. Scheidt served in this role until about 1619 or 1620. During this time, his reputation as both a composer and a performer spread. About 1614 at the latest, Scheidt came into contact with Michael Praetorius, who had been appointed as Halle's *Kapellmeister von Haus aus*[3] and occasionally directed musical groups there. One of the occasions in which Praetorius participated was the baptism of the first child of Margrave Christian Wilhelm in April 1616, at which time Praetorius conducted. In 1618 Scheidt was involved in concerts at Magdeburg with both Praetorius and Heinrich Schuetz, all three of whom had been asked to provide music in the concerted style for the cathedral there. And in 1619 when Scheidt played the dedicatory recital for the new organ in the *Stadtkirche* in Bayreuth, Praetorius, Schuetz, and Johann Staden were also present.

It is of interest to note that during this period (ca. 1610–ca. 1620) the *Hofkapelle* of which Scheidt was a member consisted of 10 instrumentalists: four trumpeters, one lutenist, one violinist, one violist, two wind instrumentalists, and one organist (Scheidt). It was near the end of this decade that the Thirty Years War (1618–48) broke out—a war which would have a marked deleterious effect on both Scheidt's personal and professional life. The specific effects of the war on Halle, however, were still a few years off.

In 1619 or 1620 Scheidt was promoted to the post of *Hofkapellmeister* in Halle, a position in which—while retaining his position as organist— he found himself in charge of an excellent group of singers and instrumentalists. The nucleus of the choral group was the group of singers from the Gymnasium; the soloists were members of the *Hofkantorei* proper. Scheidt also augmented the instrumental group that now consisted of two violinists, two violists, two performers on bass instruments, a cornettist, and an organist.

The period of the early 1620s saw the publication of a number of significant works by Scheidt that reflect both the influences of his early training as well as the direction his work would take in the future. In general Scheidt's vocal music consisted of three types: the motet, large-scale polychoral concertos for voices and instruments, and the few-voiced concertatos for a small number of voices and instruments.

Scheidt's first publication, belonging to the first of these categories, was the *Cantiones sacrae* (1620), motets set for eight voices without *basso continuo,* published in Hamburg, and dedicated to Christian Wilhelm. These 39 settings of both Latin and German texts in the older polychoral style reflect the influence of Orlando di Lasso and the Italian *prima prattica* and developed out of the practices in the services at Halle.

---

[3] A largely honorary position requiring only infrequent appearances by Michael Praetorius at the court.

These double-chorus motets, mostly based on psalms or liturgical texts and nearly half of them based on Lutheran chorales, were a significant contribution to the development of the choral motet (Ex. 43). In imitation of his organ variations, Scheidt gives each verse of the chorale a different setting, arriving at a chain of contrapuntal variations, a practice which forms one of the roots of the chorale cantata. While only one of the pieces specifically indicates the use of instruments (two clarinos in "In dulci jubilo"), it is entirely likely that Scheidt envisioned the occasional use of instruments doubling voice parts, a not uncommon practice throughout the Renaissance. This collection is a kind of parallel publication to the *Cymbalum Sionium* of Schein published only five years earlier in 1615.

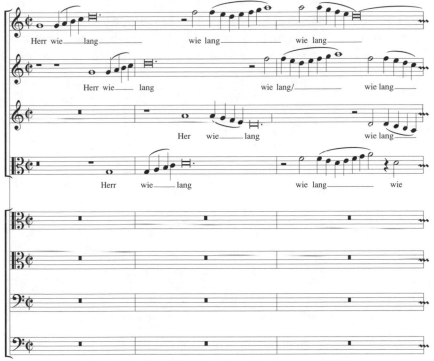

Ex. 43. Samuel Scheidt, "Herr wie lang" from *Cantiones sacrae* (1620)

The *Concerti sacri 2–12 voc. adjectis symphoniis et choris instrumentalibus* (1622) reflects the influence of the new Venetian style in its colorful settings for solo ensembles, echo choruses, and instrumental sinfonias. This work contained 12 compositions: four psalms, three Magnificats, a parody Mass (on the eight-part setting of Psalm 8), and four other settings of liturgical texts. None of the compositions are based on Lutheran chorales, a fact that made possible a greater attempt at textual depiction apart from use of a *cantus firmus*. In Friedrich Blume's estimation, the "affect-laden melodies and pathos-laden declamation reach beyond Praetorius, but go nowhere near the intensive energy of Schein's textual declamation."[4] This work is comparable in many ways to Praetorius' *Polyhymnia caduceatrix*, yet the harmonic language of these compositions was conservative, not venturing much beyond the cadential frictions that can be found in the music of Giovanni Gabrieli. These compositions likewise developed out of the services at Halle.

By contrast Scheidt's *Ludi musici* (1621/22/25/27), a collection of 32 instrumental dance movements, reflects the secular court music of the time. Intended as entertainment music at dinner, this collection consisted of *paduana*, *galliarda*, *courante*, *allemande*, *intrada*, and *canzonetto* in four and five parts with *basso continuo* for string or wind instruments (Ex. 44). The movements, generally grouped by dance type and not grouped in suites, form an interesting parallel and contrast both to Praetorius' *Terpsichore* (1612) and Schein's *Banchetto musicale* (1617).

Ex. 44. Samuel Scheidt, "Courant" from *Ludi musici* (1621 ff)

Above all, it is in Scheidt's contributions to the development of organ music, particularly organ music for the Lutheran service, and in his turn from the old organ tablature to the "new tablature"—each part written on a separate staff—that he is most prominently remembered. Scheidt's magnum opus, the *Tabulatura nova* (1624), was published in three parts exactly one hundred years after the publication of the first Lutheran hymnbook.[5] Part I contains variations on German chorales and secular airs, fan-

---

    [4] Friedrich Blume, *Protestant Church Music: A History* (New York: W. W. Norton & Co., 1974), 205.

    [5] Both the *Etlich Cristlich lider* (the so-called *Achtliederbuch*) and Johann Walter's *Geystliche gesangk Buchleyn* were published in 1524.

tasias in fugal style, and canons. It is interesting to note that the very first piece in this entire work—as it would be in his later *Newe geistliche Conzerten*—is a setting of the Lutheran Credo, "Wir glauben all' an einen Gott" (Ex. 45). Part II contains fugues, variations, works employing echo devices, a fantasia on a theme by Sweelinck, and toccatas, among other works. In this second part, only one work is based on a Latin hymn. In these first two volumes, all eight sets of variations are based on

Ex. 45. Samuel Scheidt, "Wir glauben all' an einen Gott" from *Tabulatura nova I* (1624)

Lutheran chorales. Part III of the *Tabulatura nova* was prepared specifically for use in the liturgical services of the Lutheran church and thus contains no secular music.

With only one exception, all the material included in Part III is based on Latin liturgical *cantus firmi*. It contains those portions of the liturgy that the organist in Halle was required to play or in which the organist participated. Included is material for the Holy Communion as well as for Matins and Vespers. Following settings of the Kyrie and Gloria, one finds nine organ settings of the Magnificat, that is, *alternatim* settings of the even-numbered verses, the other verses to be sung by cantor or choir (Ex. 46). After the hymns for Vespers, one finds settings of the Credo. Scheidt

Ex. 46. Samuel Scheidt, "Et exultavit" from *Tabulatura nova III* (1624)

also provides specific suggestions for the performer, including the specific mention that the *cantus firmus* is to be clear, distinct, and to be played when possible with a clear solo stop.[6] The different "verses" of the chorale could be used—like the Catholic versets—in the practice of alternation, a common practice in Lutheran worship of the time. The number of varia-

---

[6] "Scheidt specifies that on an organ with two manuals and pedal this voice should be played on the Rueckpositiv 'with a piercing sound, so that the chorale can be heard more distinctly', or on the pedal using a 4' stop if the chorale is in the alto." See Kerala J. Snyder, "Scheidt, Samuel," in vol. 16 of *The New Grove Dictionary of Music and Musicians* (ed. Stanley Sadie; New York: Macmillan, 1980), 400.

tions did not necessarily coincide with the number of stanzas, nor was there any particular relation between the musical patterns of a particular variation and the words of a specific stanza. The very idea of a subjective musical interpretation of the chorale text was quite foreign to the early Baroque organist. It was the organist's role simply to "present" the chorale in purely abstract elaboration. Scheidt's work in the *Tabulatura nova* shows the infinite possibilities of combining a variety of abstract patterns with a *cantus firmus*. Each phrase of the chorale is often set off through the use of a different rhythmic idea. Bukofzer summarizes Scheidt's approach in the following way:

> In his extended variations Scheidt sharpened the contrast between the chorale melody and the abstract patterns of the other voices in order to emphasize the structural function of the cantus firmus and to make it as prominent as possible. The musical style was directly bound up with the baroque organ, minutely described by Praetorius in his *Syntagma musicum*.[7]

The *Tabulatura nova* was "new" because instead of the old-fashioned German tablature, Scheidt adopted the new Italian practice of writing out each voice on a separate staff. This work was a milestone in the development of organ literature as well as a volume providing significant insights into the use of the organ in Lutheran worship of the period.

While Christhard Mahrenholz is of the opinion that the conclusion of Scheidt's activities as an active organist may have coincided with the publication of the *Tabulatura nova*, it is clear that his interest in the organ continued. In 1624/25, the young Compenius built an organ for the *Moritzkirche* under Scheidt's supervision. Scheidt was also asked repeatedly to examine organs in such cities as Leipzig, Gera, and Altenburg, and his reports and opinions reveal a thorough knowledge and understanding of the technical side of the organ builder's craft.

By 1625 the tensions of the Thirty Years War were becoming more acute in Halle. After some deliberation, Christian Wilhelm decided to ally himself with Christian IV of Denmark. In November 1625, Wallenstein took over most of the city, Christian Wilhelm left, and court life ceased to function. Most of the court musicians left to find employment elsewhere. In 1630 Gustavus Adolphus took over the city amid general rejoicing, but it was not until 1644 that Halle once again became the official center of the court and court life.

In the midst of the war, at the age of 40, Samuel Scheidt married Helena Magdalena Keller on April 15, 1627. His wife was the daughter of a citizen of Halle who was also a member of the town council. The mar-

---

[7] Bukofzer, op. cit., 105.

riage, which took place in nearby Woermlich, was blessed with seven children, four of whom died in the plague of 1636.

In 1628, the year following his marriage, Scheidt became director of music of the city of Halle, an invitation most likely prompted by the city's desire to retain the services of this famous musician. This post afforded Scheidt the opportunity to reform the music program of the city and to introduce the new concerted style into the *schola* and in the principal church of St. Mary. Two years later, however, Scheidt was forced to give up this position as a result of continuing disagreements regarding his position in relation to the school and its administration.

The years after 1630 saw the appearance of a number of important new works of Scheidt. Chief among them was the *Liebliche Kraftbluemlein, aus dem Heiligen Geistes Lustgarten abgebrochen und zum Vorschmack des ewigen Lebens in zweistimmigen Himmelschor versetzt* (1635) (*Lovely, Fragrant Little Flowers from the Pleasure Garden of the Holy Spirit, Set for a Two-Part Heavenly Choir as a Foretaste of Eternal Life*), a collection of 12 pieces in concerto style for two voices and general-bass, which Blume dismissively describes as "fully as pretentious as its title, its style abounds in superficial musical effects and concerted triflings . . ."[8]

The *Newe geistliche Conzerten*, which appeared in four parts (1631/34/35/40), contained a variety of settings of church hymns, psalms, Magnificats, and other biblical texts set for two to six voices with *basso continuo*. Part I begins, as noted earlier, with a setting of "Wir glauben all' an einen Gott" for three voices with *basso continuo* (Ex. 47).

Ex. 47. Samuel Scheidt, "Wir glauben all' an einen Gott" from *Newe geistliche Conzerten I* (1631)

Apparently the original form of these compositions was for several choirs with *obbligato* instruments and instrumental sinfonias. The problem of the availability of the necessary forces caused by the Thirty Years War appar-

---

[8] Blume, op. cit., 206.

ently resulted in Scheidt's reworking these large-scale pieces for solo voices with *basso continuo*. In these pieces, Scheidt more nearly approximates the more subjective interpretations of Schein, yet as Blume points out, Scheidt's interest in this form was more directed toward the formal structure rather than as a vehicle for affective textual treatment. A setting of the Passion hymn "Herzlich tut mich verlangen" from Part IV (Ex. 48) reflects this tendency, as well as shows Scheidt's continuing affection for the chorale.

Ex. 48. Samuel Scheidt, "Herzlich tut mich verlangen" from *Newe geistliche Conzerten IV* (1640)

The changing fortunes of the city of Halle under the Swedes and the Saxons had brought the city to ruin. The plague that ravaged much of central Germany had resulted in the death of four of Scheidt's children in 1636. However, about 1638 Halle began to experience gradual relief from the pestilence and plundering of the war. The administrator Christian Wilhelm was deposed, and with the accession of Prince August of Saxony to the post of administrator, the picture began to brighten both for the city and for Scheidt. Soon after the festive service of welcome for the new regent, for which he had written a well-received Te Deum, Scheidt was reinstated as *Kapellmeister* of the Halle court. It was not until 1644, however—the year in which the administrator took up residence in Halle—that the city again became the center of court life. In this same year, the 70 *Symphonien auff Concerten manir* (1644) appeared, a set of 70 "symphonies" for three parts (two treble parts and one bass part) and *basso continuo*, 10 in each of seven keys, to be used as introductions, or *ritornellos*, for the various concerted works which might be performed by choral and instrumental groups. (See Ex. 49.) The work was dedicated to Prince August of Saxony. Also from this same time is a collection of more than 100 five-part sacred madrigals (probably a counterpart to Schein's *Israelsbruennlein* of 1623), which Scheidt had promised to deliver to the Duke of Brunswick in 1642, but which unfortunately has been lost.

Meanwhile the Thirty Years War was drawing to a close. Halle was spared the ravages of the final years of the war. With the close of the war in 1648, Scheidt once again turned to music for the organ. His last publication was his *Tabulaturbuch, 100 geistliche Lieder und Psalmen . . . fuer die Herren Organisten* (1650), the so-called *Goerlitzer Tabulaturbuch,* dedicated to the town of Goerlitz as a token of gratitude to the town council, which had agreed to subsidize its publication. The collection contained 100 four-part chorales in open score (as in the *Tabulatura nova*) with *cantus firmus* in the upper voice, ordered according to the church

Ex. 49. Samuel Scheidt, "Symphony" from *70 Symphonien auff Concerten manir* (1644)

Fig. 13. View of the city of Halle

year and Luther's catechism. (See Ex. 50.) The settings in this collection, Scheidt says in the foreword to this publication, were "for organists to play with Christian congregations"—that is, they were used not as accompaniment for congregational singing, but as organ settings in alternation with the singing of the chorales by the congregation.[9]

Ex. 50. Samuel Scheidt, "Aus tiefer Not" from *Tabulaturbuch* (1650)

Scheidt continued to live in Halle until his death on Good Friday, March 24, 1654. Among his many students, only Adam Krieger achieved a more lasting fame. Scheidt's importance to church music may be found in that he was the first to treat the chorale in a manner artistically and idiomatically suited to the organ. He became the founder and guiding spirit of the Central German School of organ music. His moderate and somewhat conventional vocal style was not unlike that of many of his contemporaries, and on the whole, Scheidt was more conservative and moderate than Schein. Blume's evaluation of his work is as follows:

> In Scheidt arose the type of Lutheran church musician who endeavored with sound, traditional craftsmanship to unite the new and the old, thereby supplying models that easily became stereotyped in the hands of a wider circle of followers.[10]

---

[9] This statement in the foreword has been interpreted, mistakenly, to mean that this collection was intended to accompany the congregation. See Paul Henry Lang, *Music in Western Civilization* (New York: W. W. Norton & Co., 1941), 400.

[10] Blume, op.cit., 207.

Scheidt was perhaps somewhat more musically conservative than Schein, a fact that he confesses in a letter to Baryphonus in 1651, in which he says, "I stick to the pure old compositions and standards."[11] Nevertheless, Scheidt continued to explore many of the new musical forms and devices that were emerging in his day. That Scheidt was a pious man of strong character, loyal to the Lutheran church, her teachings and traditions, is clearly evident as one studies his life and music. Of his love for the chorale, perhaps no one speaks on Scheidt's behalf better than Walter E. Buszin.

> We may also be sure that he loved the chorales of his church; he used them to so great an extent that we cannot think of his music without thinking of the chorale . . . The chorales were to him an expression of his Christian faith, and it was hardly accidental that the first opus of each of his two most monumental works, the *Tabulatura nova* and his *Geistliche Konzerte*, was a composition based on the Lutheran Credo: *Wir glauben all' an einen Gott.* [12]

Samuel Scheidt was a transitional figure who exemplifies in his own music the movement from the older style of the Lassus school to the newer techniques, devices, and spirit of the emerging Baroque period. As the "father of German organ music" and in his use of and love for the chorale, Scheidt has earned a lasting place in the development of Lutheran church music in the period between Martin Luther and Johann Sebastian Bach.

---

[11] Quoted by Blume, op. cit., 206.

[12] Walter E. Buszin, "The Life and Work of Samuel Scheidt," in vol. V of *The Musical Heritage of the Church* (ed. Theodore Hoelty-Nickel; St. Louis: Concordia, 1959), 67.

SAMUEL SCHEIDT

| 1580 | 1590 | 1600 | 1610 | 1620 | 1630 | 1640 | 1650 | 1660 |

Cantiones sacrae (1620)

Ludi musici (1621 ff)

Concerti sacri (1622)

Tabulatura nova (1624)

Newe geistliche Conzerten (1631 ff)

Liebliche Kraftbluemlein (1635)

70 Symphonien auff Concerten manir (1644)

Tabulaturbuch, 100 geistliche Lieder und Psalmen (1650)

Guide to Samuel Scheidt's Collected Works

Scheidt, Samuel. *Werke* (*SW*). Edited by Gottlieb Harms and Christhard Mahrenholz. Currently 16 vols. Hamburg: Ugrino Verlag. 1923—. (In progress).

1620   *Cantiones sacrae* (*SW* 4)

A collection of 39 settings of Latin and German texts for two choirs (eight parts) without *basso continuo* in the older polychoral style. Most texts are from the psalms or the liturgy.

1621ff   *Ludorum musicorum* (*Ludi musici*) (*SW* 2, 3)

A collection of 32 instrumental dance settings (*paduana, galliarda, courante, allemande, intrada,* and *canzonetto*) in four and five parts with *basso continuo*.

1622   *Concerti sacri* (*SW* 14, 15)

Edited by Hans Gruess. Twelve concerted works (four psalms, three Magnificats, a parody Mass on the eight-part setting of Psalm 8, and four other settings of liturgical texts) for two to eight voices and instruments with figured bass.

1624   *Tabulatura nova*

Edited by Christhard Mahrenholz. Keyboard settings published in three parts. Part I (*SW* 6): three *Cantio sacra;* three *Fantasias;* one *Passamezzo;* two *Courantes;* two *Neiderlaendisch Liedchen;* one *Franzoesisch Liedchen;* 24 three- to five-voice canons. Part II (*SW* 6): two *Fuga;* one echo; two *Cantio sacra* on German hymns; one *Fantasia;* one *Hymnus;* five variations on "Cantilena Angelica de Fortuna"; eight verses on "Gelobet seiest du, Jesu Christ." Part III (*SW* 7): one Kyrie; one Credo; one Psalmus (for Communion on "Jesus Christus, unser Heiland"); six Hymnus on Latin hymns; nine Magnificats; two studies for manuals and double pedal; and a section giving suggestions for registration.

The *Tabulatura nova* is also found in *Denkmaeler deutscher Tonkunst.* 1. Folge vol. 1. Edited by Max Seiffert; new and critical edition by Hans Joachim Moser.

1631/1634
1635/1640 *Newe geistliche Conzerten*
    Edited by Christhard Mahrenholz (Part I); Christhard
    Mahrenholz and Adam Adrio (Part II); Adam Adrio (Part III);
    and Erika Gessner (Part IV).
    Twenty few-voiced concertos with *basso continuo*. Part I
    (*SW* 8): German texts set for two to eight voices with *contin-*
    uo, including church hymns, psalms, and liturgical pieces.
    Part II (*SW* 9): 30 settings for three to six voices with *contin-*
    uo; 28 have German texts, two have Latin texts. Part III (*SW*
    10, 11): German (19) and Latin (15) hymns arranged accord-
    ing to the church year for two to to six voices with *basso con-*
    tinuo; includes three Magnificats for Christmas, Easter, and
    Pentecost with related seasonal texts interpolated between the
    verses of the canticle. Part IV (*SW* 12): 31 German hymns for
    two to six voices with *basso continuo.*

1635   *Liebliche Kraftbluemlein* (*SW* 16)
    Edited by Erika Gessner. Twelve settings for two voices
    with *basso continuo* in concerto style. One setting is based on
    a hymn text, 11 on biblical texts.

1644   *70 Symphonien auff Concerten manir* (*SW* 13)
    Edited by Christhard Mahrenholz and Hermann Keller. Ten
    preludes in each of seven keys set for three instrumental parts
    (two treble, one bass part) with *continuo*. Designed for use as
    introductions to concertos.

1650   *Tabulaturbuch, 100 geistliche Lieder und Psalmen* (*SW* 1)
    One hundred organ chorales in four parts, *cantus firmus* in
    the upper voice, arranged according to the church year and
    designed for use in the alternate singing of hymns.

* * * * * * *

Keyboard music not included in the above collections—including toccatas, variations on hymn melodies, and variations on *galliarda, bergam-*
asca, and a *Niederlaendisches Lied*—may be found in *SW* 5.

Selected References for Further Reading

Primary Sources:
Scheidt, Samuel. *Tabulatura nova.* Edited by Harold Vogel. 2 vols. Wiesbaden: Breitkopf & Härtel, 1994–99.
Scheidt, Samuel. *Werke.* Edited by Gottlieb Harms and Christhard Mahrenholz. Currently 16 vols. Hamburg: Ugrino Verlag. 1923—. (In progress).

Secondary Sources:
Buszin, Walter E. "The Life and Work of Samuel Scheidt." Pages 43–67 in vol. V of *The Musical Heritage of the Church.* Edited by Theodore Hoelty-Nickel. St. Louis: Concordia, 1959.
Mahrenholz, Christhard. *Samuel Scheidt.* Leipzig: Breitkopf & Haertel, 1924.
————. "Scheidt, Samuel." Cols. 1627–40 in vol. 11 of *Die Musik in Geschichte und Gegenwart.* Kassel u. Basel: Baerenreiter, 1963.
Serauky, Walter. *Samuel Scheidt in seinen Briefen.* Halle: Gebauer-Schwetschke Verlag, 1937.
Snyder, Kerala J. "Scheidt, Samuel." Pages 604–11 in vol. 16 of *The New Grove Dictionary of Music and Musicians.* Edited by Stanley Sadie. New York: Macmillan, 1980.

8

Heinrich Schuetz

Tone Poet of Saxony

A t the height of the Renaissance, 15 years before the end of the 16th century and exactly 100 years before the birth of Johann Sebastian

Fig. 14. Rembrandt's portrait of a musician (1633), probably Heinrich Schuetz

Bach, Heinrich Schuetz was born in the little town of Koestritz, about three miles from Gera in what is now Saxony. Just as the towering figure of Schuetz—whose music has been more and more appreciated in recent years—has tended to obscure the significant contributions of his predecessors from Walter to Scheidt, so Schuetz's musical achievements have tended to exist in the shadow cast by the even greater achievements of Bach. Schuetz's contribution to the shaping of the Lutheran musical tradition, particularly in his sensitive and often dramatic expression of the sense of the text in his music, cannot be overestimated. Noted for the variety of his musical output, his adoption of Italian monody—true solo as opposed to choral song—into the orbit of German polyphony stands as a lasting contribution to the development of music in Germany.

Baptized on October 9, 1585, Heinrich Schuetz was the second child and the oldest son in the family of Christoph Schuetz, innkeeper of *Zum goldenen Kranich* in Koestritz, and Euphosina Bieger, daughter of the mayor of Gera and Christoph's second wife. The Schuetz family was highly respected and active in both business and politics.[1] Schuetz's aunt Justina was the mother of Heinrich Albert (1604–51), the noted poet and hymn writer. Two of Heinrich's younger brothers became well-known

---

[1] Schuetz's father, who later became mayor of Weissenfels, served as a town clerk in Gera in the mid-1570s. He then took over the inn *Zum goldenen Kranich* at Koestritz, which had been owned by his father.

jurists. The family was noted for a number of important merchants and civil servants who originally came from Nuremberg.

Schuetz's Early Life

In the late summer of 1590, when the young Heinrich was not quite five years old, the family moved to Weissenfels, where they lived at the *Haus zum goldenen Ring,* which Christoph had inherited from his father. Christoph also purchased a second inn, which he renamed the *Gasthof zum Schuezen.* It was here at Weissenfels as a young boy that Schuetz listened to the organist Heinrich Colander and heard the local church choir in hymns arranged for two choirs under the direction of Georg Weber, the choirmaster who had been educated in Wittenberg. It is very likely that at some time the young Heinrich sang in this church choir where "in a short time he had learned to sing accurately and quite well, with a special charm,"[2] according to Martin Geier, who delivered the sermon at Schuetz's funeral.

In 1598, when Landgrave Moritz von Hessen Cassel happened to spend the night at the home of Schuetz's parents and heard the boy sing, "His Grace was moved to suggest to the parents that they allow the boy to accompany him to his court, promising that he would be educated in all good arts and praiseworthy virtues."[3] While his parents were initially reluctant, the Landgrave persisted. In August 1599, just a few months shy of his 14th birthday, young Heinrich became a choirboy in the court chapel at Cassel and a pupil at the *Collegium Mauritiarum*, a school founded by Moritz in 1595. At this school, "amidst counts, noblemen, and other valorious *ingena*, [Schuetz] was brought up to study various languages, arts, and *exercitia*, for which his industrious, keen mind and intellectual appetite prepared him well."[4] The conductor at the court chapel

---

[2] Quoted in Hans Joachim Moser, *Heinrich Schuetz: His Life and Work* (trans. Carl F. Pfatteicher from the 2d rev. ed.; St. Louis: Concordia, 1959), 27. This volume, despite some corrections and reevaluations of aspects of Schuetz's life and work since the first appearance of this book, remains the most magisterial treatment of Schuetz. See also the biographical information provided by Martin Geier in his funeral sermon for Schuetz in Robin A. Leaver, *Music in the Service of the Church: The Funeral Sermon for Heinrich Schuetz (1585–1672),* Church Music Pamphlet Series (ed. Carl Schalk; St. Louis: Concordia, 1984), which originally appeared in *Bach: The Quarterly Journal of the Riemenschneider Bach Institutue* iv/4 (1973): 3; v/1 (1974): 9; v/2 (1974): 22; v/3 (1974): 13.

[3] Ibid.

[4] Martin Geier, quoted by Leo Schrade in "Heinrich Schuetz and Johann Sebastian Bach in the Protestant Liturgy," in vol. VII of *The Musical Heritage of the Church* (ed. Theodore Hoelty-Nickel; St. Louis: Concordia, 1970), 171.

was Georg Otto, who had been born in Torgau and who, as a boy, had studied at the Torgau Latin School, where he sang under the direction of Johann Walter, first cantor of the Lutheran church. Otto, who must be considered Schuetz's first formal music teacher, was a composer of no small ability. Among Otto's compositions was a set of *Cantiones sacrae* for five and six voices, various settings of psalms for eight to 10 voices, and—his chief work—a series of Gospel settings for the church year for four to eight voices. His essentially linear, imitative style brings him close to such other German composers as Seth Calvisius, Gallus Dressler, and Leonhard Schroeter. It was amid such music that Schuetz grew and flourished.

The musical life at the court was particularly attractive. Moritz himself could compose music. Among his compositions are his own melodies and settings for every psalm in the *Lobwasser Psalter*, Magnificats in each of the 12 modes, instrumental fugues, *villanellas*, motets, and intradas. In addition, he invited a wide variety of musicians, such as John Dowland and Michael Praetorius, to the court. Moritz placed great stress on musical instruction and encouraged his pupils to devote themselves wholeheartedly to their studies. Moreover, the music inventory of the court chapel contained pieces by an astonishing variety of the most significant composers of the past and present.[5] It was in the midst of such a stimulating environment that Heinrich Schuetz first developed his skills and interest in what was to be his life's vocation.

The Years in Venice (1609–13)

As Schuetz recalled in later years, "after I had lost my soprano voice" and had very likely served several more years at the court assisting as a male singer, instrumentalist, and organist of the *Kantorei,* at the urging of his parents, Schuetz entered the University of Marburg in 1609 to study law. Although some have suggested that he may also have studied briefly at Frankfurt an der Oder and in Jena between the years 1603–07, there is no evidence. Apparently in these early years, while music was an interest of the young Schuetz, it was the study of law that was uppermost in his mind.

Landgrave Moritz, however, was more and more convinced that the young Schuetz should study further in music. In 1609, on a visit to Marburg, Moritz suggested to Schuetz that "since the world-famous Johann Gabrieli of Venice was still alive, he would be inclined, in case Schuetz looked upon the suggestion favorably, to give him the necessary

---

[5] For a listing of the composers included in the court chapel library, see Moser, op. cit., 35.

funds and send him to Italy in order that he might seriously continue the study of music there."[6] Schuetz accepted the offer and left for Venice—the foremost musical city of that day—to study with Giovanni Gabrieli. To help pay his expenses, the Landgrave gave him an annual stipend of 200 thalers, apparently for a period of two years.

The years in Venice exposed Schuetz to the excitement and vitality of a great city that stood at the center of many of the period's musical developments. At the focal point of his experience was the tutelage of Gabrieli, which developed into a close relationship between pupil and teacher, an affection illustrated by the fact that some years later, on his deathbed, Gabrieli bequeathed to his pupil a ring as a memento of their friendship.

In these years, Schuetz's first published work appeared, the *Il primo libro de madrigali*, his so-called *Italian Madrigals,* a set of 18 secular pieces for five voices and one madrigal set for two four-part choirs. It was written as a kind of graduation exercise from his studies. Published by the prestigious publisher Gardano in Venice in 1611, these works were without *basso continuo* and were an attempt by Schuetz's teacher to demonstrate that his pupil had mastered the skill of contrapuntal technique. Both daring and modern, these madrigals are worthy of being compared with such expressionistic composers of the time as Monteverdi and Gesualdo. It is interesting and instructive to compare the very first madrigal in Schuetz's collection, set to the text "O primavera" (Ex. 51), with the setting of the same text by Claudio Monteverdi, 18 years Schuetz's senior

Ex. 51. Heinrich Schuetz, "O primavera" from *Italian Madrigals* (1611)

---

[6] Moser, op. cit., 50.

and with whom he would come into contact on his second visit to Venice. Encouraged to continue his study, Schuetz remained in Venice an additional year at his father's expense until the death of Gabrieli in 1612. Schuetz returned to his native country and resumed his service at Moritz's court, according to his own testimony, in 1613. His years in Venice were to have a profound effect on Schuetz's future composition and would, some years later, bring him back to this city for further study because it was at the hub of many of the new musical developments of his time.

Cassel (1613–17) and Dresden (1617–28)

Upon his return to Germany, Schuetz went to Cassel, where Landgrave Moritz had created the post of second organist at the court chapel expressly for Schuetz. On a visit to Dresden in 1613 in the company of Landgrave Moritz, Schuetz came to the attention of the Elector of Saxony and made a very favorable impression as the director of one of the choirs in polychoral works under the renowned Michael Praetorius, the "visiting music director" (*Kapellmeister von Haus aus*). Elector Johann Georg I made several subsequent requests for Schuetz's services. Finally, as a result of increasing pressure brought to bear on both Schuetz and Landgrave Moritz, Schuetz left Cassel for Dresden in 1615 for what was to be a two-year appointment, but which would keep him in Dresden until 1627. In the early years after his arrival in Dresden, Schuetz served as *Kapellmeister* to Johann Georg, though at first the official title was given to Rogier Michael and Michael Praetorius remained available to direct the *Kapelle* on special occasions.

Thus at the age of 30, Schuetz in effect became the director of what was generally acknowledged to be the finest group of musicians in the Lutheran Church in Germany at the Dresden court. This was the same establishment which had been organized by Johann Walter in 1548 and which had subsequently been led by other important musicians such as Matthaeus le Maistre, Antonio Scandello, Giovanni Battista Pinello, Georg Forster, and Rogier Michael. Schuetz's responsibilities were to provide music for the various religious, social, and political occasions at the court, as well as to keep the *Kapelle* properly staffed, ensure adequate living conditions for its members, and oversee the musical education of the choirboys. That he took these responsibilities seriously is reflected in his letters, which show his continuing concern for his musicians.

Early in his tenure at Dresden, Schuetz published his *Psalmen Davids* (1619), a collection of 26 large polychoral works using Martin Luther's translation, which clearly reflected the Italian influence generally and the impact of his study with Gabrieli in particular. (See Ex. 52, a portion of

Ex. 52. Heinrich Schuetz, "Psalm 150" from *Psalmen Davids* (1619)

Schuetz's setting of Psalm 150.) The style of this collection is reflected in Schuetz's words from the preface:

> Since I have set these Psalms in the *stilo* recitative which until now has been almost unknown in Germany, and since the Psalms, having many words, call for a continuous declamation without long repetition, I would ask those who are unfamiliar with this style to be sure not to hurry the beat. It would be best to adhere to a moderate tempo, so that the words may be clearly understood. Otherwise, there will ensue a most unpleasant harmony, all too much like a battaglia di mosche [a battle of flies] and wholly at variance with the composer's intention.[7]

On June 1, 1619, Schuetz married the 18-year-old daughter of a court accountant, Magdalena Wildeck, a marriage that produced two daughters (Anna Justina and Euphrosina) but which was tragically short-lived. Magdalena died in 1625 at the age of 24. It was a tragedy which Schuetz carried with him throughout his life; he never remarried, and feeling unable to care for his daughters himself, placed them in the care of his deceased wife's mother.

Schuetz's *Historia der . . . Auferstehung . . . Jesu Christi* (*Resurrection History*) (1623)—a miniature Easter oratorio of sorts for solo voices, choir, instruments, and *basso continuo*—appeared during these years. The parts of the evangelist, Jesus, Mary Magdalene, and the young men of Emmaus are sung by solo voices—the part of Christ being set for a small ensemble of alto and tenor with *basso continuo*—singing a rather free kind of chant, accompanied by a set of viols. The choruses are for a six-part choir and two four-part choirs. The evangelist is accompanied either by the organ or by four viols called on to extemporize the accompaniment to a certain extent. It is interesting to note that Schuetz expresses his preference that in the performance of the *Resurrection History* only the evangelist should be visible to the congregation, the other performers being hidden from view.[8]

Schuetz's *Cantiones sacrae* (1625)—40 Latin motets in four parts with *basso continuo* written mostly in the older polyphonic style—also belongs

---

[7] See Erich H. Mueller, ed., *Heinrich Schuetz: Gesammelte Briefe und Schriften* (Regensburg: Gustav Bosse, 1931), 64. For the English translation, see Sam Morgenstern, ed., *Composers on Music* (New York: Pantheon Books, 1956), 27.

[8] *Es were zwar noch viel zuerindern auss was massen diese* Histori *mit besser* gratia *oder anmuth* musiciert *werden koendte, wann nehmlich der Evangelist allein gesehen wuerde, die andern Personen alle verborgen stuenden, und was mehr dergleichen ist.* See Basil Smallman, *Schuetz, The Master Musicians* (Oxford: Oxford University Press, 2000), 136.

to this period. Some of these motets have an optional *basso continuo*, while in others it is obligatory. Half of the texts are from the psalms, half from the prayer book of Andreas Musculus, with the addition of five table prayers intended for use by the choirboys. The "Blessing before eating" ("Oculi omnium in te sperant, domine"), Ex. 53, is one of these table graces that is widely sung.

Ex. 53. Heinrich Schuetz, "Oculi omnium in te sperant, domine" from *Cantiones sacrae* (1625)

In an attempt to ease his grief at the untimely death of his young wife, Schuetz set about working on setting the metrical psalm texts by the Leipzig theologian Cornelius Becker, a project that resulted in the so-called *Becker Psalter*, that appeared in 1628. These settings, several of which had been originally written for the morning and evening devotions of the choirboys in Schuetz's charge, were four-part cantional settings for voices that could be sung by small vocal ensembles or solo voice with *basso continuo*. With the exception of 13 settings based on traditional Lutheran chorale melodies[9] that had apparently become so well-established that they would hardly call for new tunes, the melodies of the *Becker Psalter* were Schuetz's own. Describing his procedure in this collection, Schuetz notes the following:

First, since I had to follow the manner of the old church tunes and yet com-

---

[9] These 13 included seven texts by Martin Luther: "Ach Gott, vom Himmel," "Es spricht der unweisen Mund," "Ein feste Burg ist unser Gott," "Es woll uns Gott," "Waer Gott nicht mit uns," "Wohl dem, der in Gottes Furcht steht," and "Aus tiefer Not." The five additional chorales were "In dich hab' ich," "Erbarm dich mein," "Nun lob, mein Seel," "Wo Gott zum Haus," and "An Wasserfluessen Babylon."

ply with the requirements of the music of today, I did not always use double-whole and whole notes, but mostly half-, quarter-, and eighth-notes. Thus, the singing will not only be more lively, but the words less protracted, better understood, and the psalm sooner finished. These faster notes, if sung according to the present fashion in their proper beat, will not detract from the gravity of the song; even the old church tunes, though rotated in long notes, are now being sung with a faster beat in Christian assemblies.

Second, instead of rests, I have used a comma after each verse because, in this kind of composition, the rests are not strictly observed, and such arias and melodies can be sung with more grace when they follow the meaning of the words. However, if someone should find these melodies too secular, or if a composer or organist wishes to use them for a chorale, he may set the descant (the chief part) to longer notes and interpose rests.[10]

This collection was in effect a Lutheran counterpart to Ambrosius Lobwasser's Reformed psalter, which was widely circulated in Germany. In this collection, Schuetz retained the modal character and rhythmic irregularity characteristic of the early Lutheran chorales at a time when the development of the hymn tune in Lutheranism was beginning to move toward the use of isorhythmic forms. This collection represented a masterful economy of expression which avoided any overly subjective means to accomplish its purpose. (Ex. 54a and 54b compare the setting of Psalm 23 in the original edition of 1628 with that of Schuetz's later revision of 1661.)

[10] See Mueller, op. cit., 82. English translation in Morgenstern, op. cit., 28.

Ex. 54a. Heinrich Schuetz, "Psalm 23" from *Becker Psalter* (1628)

Ex. 54b. Heinrich Schuetz, "Psalm 23" from *Becker Psalter* (1661)

During these years in Dresden, Schuetz also established close rela-tionships with musicians such as Samuel Scheidt,[11] Michael Praetorius, Johann Staden, and Johann Hermann Schein. Upon the death of Schein in 1630, Schuetz wrote a beautiful motet, "Das ist je gewisslich wahr," based on 1 Timothy 1:15. During 1628, the same year as the appearance of the *Becker Psalter,* Schuetz wrote the first German opera, *Daphne,* to Martin Opitz's translation of Rinuccini's Italian verse. It was performed in Torgau at the marriage of the Elector's oldest daughter. However, this important score, together with the music for his other staged works and ballets for the court, is lost.

Schuetz's Second Trip to Venice (1628–29)

Toward the end of the 1620s, the effects of the Thirty Years War (1618–48) began to be felt at the Electoral Court in Dresden. The musi-cians at the court were not being paid, and Schuetz himself had to petition for moneys owed him. The deteriorating conditions at the court led Schuetz to determine to return once again to Italy. Following the publica-tion of the *Becker Psalter,* and still suffering the grief of the loss of his wife, Schuetz made repeated requests of the Elector for a leave to study in Venice. Finally permission was granted, and in 1628, Schuetz returned for a second time to Venice.

The musical situation in Venice had undergone a significant change in the 15 years since Schuetz had first visited the city. According to his own words, " . . . since I came here the first time, compositions have changed a great deal. The music suitable at court for dinner, ballets, comedies, and the like, has improved and increased a great deal."[12] The leading musical figure in Venice was now Claudio Monteverdi (1567–1643), and the styl-istic emphasis had changed from the massive and monumental polychoral style of Gabrieli to a more intense, dramatic, and operatic monody which sought to express in every possible way the impact of each word of the text. Monteverdi was the leading exponent of this new development. While it is not certain that Schuetz actually studied with Monteverdi, there are some indications that he may have done so. At any rate, Monteverdi's influence could hardly have escaped Schuetz, and the music he wrote dur-ing this time increasingly reflects a new and more intensely personal style.

---

[11] Schuetz offered an opinion of Scheidt's music as "most pleasing to the ear" at the request of Wilhelm Ludwig Moser, to whom Schuetz had sent the first two volumes of Scheidt's *Tabulatura nova.* See letter of December 30, 1624, in Norman and Schrifte, op. cit., 12.

[12] In a letter of November 3, 1628, from Schuetz to Elector Johann Georg I. See Norman and Schrifte, op. cit., 13–14.

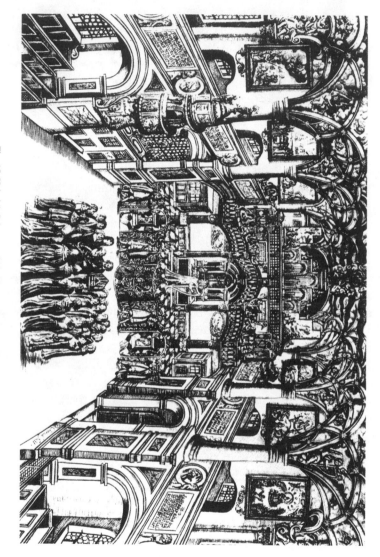

Fig. 15. Heinrich Schuetz and his *Kantorei* in the old Castle church in Dresden

Schuetz also used his time in Venice to seek out new musical scores and instruments, which he brought back with him to the court chapel in Saxony. On his return he also brought back with him Francesco Castelli, whom he engaged as leader of the orchestra for the court, and Kaspar Kittel, who had also been studying in Italy.

The Return to Dresden in 1629
and the Decline of Music at the Court

By the time of his return to Dresden at the end of 1629 and in the years following, Schuetz found that the Elector of Saxony had become increasingly involved in the Thirty Years War. The war was having an increasingly devastating effect on the musical life at the court and in the city of Dresden generally. Funds were not always available, and Schuetz often personally helped to sustain the musicians who still remained in the city, others having left to seek employment elsewhere. Repeated appeals to the Elector seemed in vain, and during the years 1633 to 1639, the Dresden court orchestra was dissolved. It was later reorganized with only 10 instruments and singers. During these years, Schuetz made frequent visits to such cities as Hamburg, Mecklenburg, Wolfenbuettel, Zeitz, Halle, and Gera where he served as conductor or musical consultant for various events. During this time, he also made several trips to Denmark—his first trip in the early 1630s, a second trip in the middle 1630s, and a third trip in 1642—where he served King Christian IV on a number of occasions. Yet it was always the court at Dresden which he served—except for the periods of time when he sought refuge in other parts of Germany or Scandinavia from the religious warfare in Dresden. Schuetz would continue to return to Dresden, and he continued to serve the court until the death of the Elector and his own semi-retirement in 1656.

Schuetz's music from the time of his second trip to Venice to the close of the Thirty Years War—the period from 1629 to 1648—reflects not only the musical developments in the post-Gabrieli period in Italy, but also the effects of the drastically reduced musical forces at his disposal as a result of the war's devastation. From this time, there issued the *Symphoniae sacrae I* (1629), published during Schuetz's last weeks in Venice. It was a collection of 20 pieces for one to three voices with several instruments and *basso continuo* using Latin texts. Eighteen years later the *Symphoniae sacrae II* (1647) appeared, which was a similar set of German concerti set for one to three voices, instruments, and *basso continuo*. (See Ex. 55.) That the texts in *Symphoniae sacrae I* were in Latin made them equally serviceable for use in either the Lutheran or the Roman Catholic liturgy. Schuetz's remarks in the preface to the second of these collections reflect

Ex. 55. Heinrich Schuetz, "Ich danke dir, Herr" from *Symphoniae sacrae II* (1647).

not only the difficulties encountered by the Thirty Years War, but, more important, the fact that this "new style" was still quite unfamiliar to many German composers. He recounts that he had written

> . . . a little Latin work for one, two and three vocal parts, accompanied by two violins or similar instruments, and within a short time it had been published in Venice under the title Symphoniae Sacrae [1619].
>
> Inasmuch as parts of the work which were imported into Germany found such favor among our musicians, and were performed in the most excellent places to German texts instead of Latin, I was spurred on to compose such a work in our German mother tongue. . . . However, until now I have been prevented from sending it to press because of the miserable conditions prevailing in our dear fatherland which adversely affect all the arts, music included;

and even more importantly, because the modern Italian style of composition and performance (with which, as the sagacious Signor Claudio Monteverdi remarks in the preface to his Eighth Book of Madrigals, music is said to have reached its final perfection) has remained largely unknown in this country.

Experience has proved that the modern Italian manner of composition and its proper tempo, with its many black notes, does not in most cases lend itself to use by Germans who have not been trained for it. Believing one had composed really good works in this style, one has often found them so violated and corrupted in performance that they offered a sensitive ear nothing but boredom and distaste, and called down unjustified opprobrium on the composer and on the German nation, the inference being that we are entirely unskilled in the noble art of music—and certain foreigners have more than once leveled such accusations at us.[13]

His *Musikalische Exequien* (1636), a burial service written for the interment of his friend Prince Heinrich Posthumus of Reuss, deserves special mention. The work is in three parts: the first is a *Missa brevis* consisting only of a substitute Kyrie and Gloria; the second is a motet for two choirs; and the third is an ethereal setting of the Nunc Dimittis in five parts while simultaneously two angel voices (sopranos) and a baritone sing the text "Blessed are the dead which die in the Lord." The choice of texts was likely made by both the prince and Schuetz together and was inscribed on the coffin in the church in Gera where the prince was buried.

Ex. 56. Heinrich Schuetz, "Erhoere mich" from *Kleine geistliche Konzerte Part I* (1636)

The other work of particular significance in this period was the two sets of *Kleine geistliche Konzerte* (1636, 1639)—24 pieces in the first book, 31 pieces in the second—for one to five solo voices with *basso continuo* and with texts generally from Luther's translation of the Bible. The smaller scale represented by these pieces made their performance possible with the more limited resources that the ravages created by the Thirty

---

[13] From the preface to the *Symphonia sacrae II* (1647). See Mueller, op. cit., 178. English translation in Morgenstern, op. cit., 28–29.

Years War had made common. The setting for "Erhoere mich" (Ex. 56) from Part I—dedicated to the head of the appellate court in Dresden, Heinrich von Friesen—for two voices and *continuo* is typical in the reduced musical forces called for and reflect the toll that the war had taken on musical life generally. The dedication reads in part:

> The way in which honorable Music, in common with the other free arts, has not only decreased as a result of the persistent dangers of war around us in our beloved Fatherland, but in many places has been completely subdued, is, with other general ruins and sudden violent disorders, apparent to many. I myself have experienced something of this on account of some musical opera which I have composed and which, for want of publishers, I have had to withhold as yet and still do, until it please the Almighty in His great mercy to grant us better times.[14]

Also at this time Schuetz requested from Ferdinand III a copyright privilege for his works which forbade the unauthorized reprinting of his musical works for a period of five years in the neighboring territories of the Holy Roman Empire, a protection he already enjoyed in Saxony.

Other works from this time worthy of particular mention include several dramatic dialogues, such as the "Vater Abraham, erbarm' dich mein" ("Father Abraham, have mercy on me") and the Easter dialogue "Weib, was weinest du" ("Woman, why weepest thou"), which represent the early advances of a quasi-oratorio style in Germany. The best example of this kind of work that one finds in Schuetz's music, however, is the miniature oratorio *Die sieben Worte Jesu Christi am Kreuz* (*The Seven Words from the Cross*, 1647) for solo voices, chorus, and instruments. It is unique for its time. Its opening chorus (in five parts) uses the traditional Lenten text "Da Jesus an dem Kreuze stund," though without the chorale melody with which it was associated (Ex. 57). The opening and closing choruses frame seven short episodes (plus two brief instrumental movements) which tell the story of the crucifixion. The story is carried by dramatic recitative and arioso-like sections. The words of Christ (Ex. 58), however, are always accompanied by violins—an early example of the technique employed in the following century by Bach in his *St. Matthew Passion*.

The final work from this general period appeared in the same year as the Treaty of Westphalia, which brought to a conclusion the Thirty Years War. It was the *Geistliche Chormusik* (1648), a collection of 29 motets for five to seven voices in a more objective style than the very personal solo works. It was dedicated to the *Thomanerchor*, the choir of St. Thomas in

---

[14] Quoted in Moser, *Heinrich Schuetz: A Short Account of His Life and Works* (trans. and ed. by Derek McCulloch; New York: St. Martin's Press, 1967), 63. Originally published in Germany under the title *Kleines Heinrich-Schuetz-Buch*.

Leipzig. In some ways these motets return to the spirit of Schuetz's early works, yet with a warmth of expression and sensitivity developed in his more mature years. They rank among the greatest works in this form that Germany has produced.

Ex. 57. Heinrich Schuetz, "Da Jesus an dem Kreuze stund" from *Die sieben Worte Jesu Christi am Kreuz* (1647)

Ex. 58. Heinrich Schuetz, from *Die sieben Worte Jesu Christi am Kreuz* (1647)

The Years in Retirement

With the conclusion of the Thirty Years War, Schuetz undoubtedly hoped for a return to the musical vitality characteristic at the court in earlier years. That this was not to be the case can be seen from repeated requests for support for the musicians at the court. Typical is a letter dated May 28, 1652, from Schuetz to Christian Reichbrodt, the privy secretary to the Elector of Saxony, Schuetz's patron:

> . . . I can no longer conceal from you that the bass singer who some time ago had to pawn his clothes again, and ever since has been living at his house like a wild beast of the woods, has informed me through his wife that he now must and wishes to leave us. . . . I leave it to your discretion whether you could procure something for him from our kind patron. . . . It is a real pity, though, to lose such an exquisite voice in the choir.[15]

Fig. 16. Oil painting of Schuetz in Leipzig by Christoph Spetner

Schuetz also repeatedly requested his superiors to relieve him of some of his duties so he could give more time to composing. After 1656 he lived, for the most part, in Weissenfels with his sister, where he found more time to compose, having been granted at least semi-retirement by Johann Georg II following the death of Elector Johann Georg I. In his retirement, for which he was granted an annual pension of 800 thalers and various other perquisites, Schuetz was required to be in Dresden only for certain formal occasions. With more time available to use as he saw fit, Schuetz was able to compose at somewhat greater leisure, though he continued to travel as time and opportunity presented itself.

These post-Thirty Years War years saw the publication of the *Symphoniae sacrae III* (1650), which contained 21 large-scale pieces for three to five voices, some with choir instruments, and occasionally a double choir. This final book of the *Symphoniae sacrae* includes perhaps the most famous pieces in the collection, Schuetz's setting of the text "Saul, Saul, was verfolgst du mich," which he wrote for the feast of the

---

[15] See Norman and Schrifte, op. cit., 14–15.

Conversion of St. Paul. The music depicts God's insistent question to Saul of Tarsus with such dramatic intensity that Hans Moser characterizes this piece as "probably the most shattering nightmare depicted in pre-classical music."[16] In 1657 there appeared the *Zwoelf geistliche Gesaenge*, a collection of nine pieces for the service, two table graces, and a hymn intended for the use of the schoolboys. The works are all for four voices and include Schuetz's setting of the Words of Institution together with a Kyrie, a German Gloria, a Magnificat, and several other pieces.

The years 1664–66 encompass the time when Schuetz's *Historia der Geburt Jesu Christi* and the three Passions according to Matthew, Luke, and John appeared. Schuetz was about 80 years old. The *Historia* (1664) is particularly interesting in its startling freshness, its handling of the recitatives—which are "no longer in the solemn, pompous *stile rappresentativo* of Florence and Venice, [but] in the lightest *parlando secco* with *basso continuo*"[17]—and its "interludes" in which specific instruments are an essential part of the entire scheme of the composition.

The three Passions, all apparently written in 1666, are the crowning glory of Schuetz's work. They are solidly rooted in the traditional dramatic *a cappella* Passions of the previous century and a half and are intended for liturgical use. They are written for chorus and solo recitatives in a plainsong style unaccompanied by *basso continuo*. It is generally assumed that the *Luke Passion* was the earliest and the *Matthew Passion* the last of the three to be written. The *Matthew Passion* is the most extensive and significant of the three. Ex. 59 demonstrates the character of Schuetz's plainsong together with the simple, brief, yet sublime chorus "Herr, bin ichs?" It remains only to mention Schuetz's *German Magnificat* for double chorus, written when he was 85 years old, and two psalm settings (119, 100), which have come down in incomplete form.

It is likely that a short time before his death, Schuetz returned to Dresden. Anticipating his death, he asked his pupil Christoph Bernhard to write a five-part motet in the style of Palestrina to the text of Psalm 119:54 ("Thy statutes have been my songs in the house of my pilgrimage."), which Schuetz received in 1670, two years before his death. On November 6, 1672, Schuetz was stricken and died peacefully amid the prayers and hymns of those who had come to his bedside. At his funeral service in the *Frauenkirche* in Dresden, four German pieces were sung: the motet of Bernhard—which, unfortunately, has been lost—and three

---

[16] Moser, *Heinrich Schuetz, A Short Account*, op. cit., 78.

[17] Ibid., 88.

Ex. 59. Heinrich Schuetz, excerpt from the *Matthew Passion* (1666)

works by Schuetz himself, though which ones are not known. The inscription written in Latin on his tomb reads as follows:

> The Christian singer of psalms, a joy for
> foreigners, a light, an immortal adornment of
> the chapel of the two electors, over which he
> presided for fifty-seven years. That which in
> him which was mortal he laid down beneath
> this monument, erected through the munificence
> of the elector, in the eighty-seventh year of
> his age, in the year 1672 of our reckoning.[18]

At Schuetz's own request, his funeral sermon,[19] delivered by Martin Geier, the Dresden court preacher, said as little as possible about the composer himself and concentrated rather on the importance of music in the service of God. Schuetz was laid to rest beside his wife, who had preceded him to the grave 47 years earlier.

---

[18] See Moser, op. cit., 225.

[19] See Leaver, op. cit. This pamphlet also contains a detailed description of the burial service.

Schuetz's best-known pupils included his cousin Heinrich Albert, Christoph Bernhard,[20] Matthias Weckmann,[21] Johann Theile,[22] and Johannes Klemm. Bernhard's *Tractatus compositionus augmentatis* is in reality an introduction to Schuetz's compositional technique, which had as its goal expressing the meaning of the text through music.[23]

Schuetz was a pathfinder, a transitional figure, one who discovered and furthered a new style, rather than one who completed and furthered an older one. His music combined the clarity and grace of the Italian style of his day with the solidity of his own German heritage, clearly setting the course which would result in the music of Bach, born just 13 years after Schuetz's death.

Schuetz's adoption of Italian monody went far beyond anything his German predecessors or contemporaries had done, and it was absorbed into his own unique style with the most profound reverence for the religious texts he set so effectively. Yet in his older years, Schuetz continued to assert the importance of the older tradition and its creative continuance, not only in such compositions as his Passion settings, but in his insistence that the younger generation of composers and musicians establish a firm grounding in polyphony. His insistence on a firm grounding in the "old style"—as opposed to what some saw as the decorative bombast of the concerted style—is seen nowhere more clearly than in the preface to his *Geistliche Chormusik* (1648).

> . . . no musician trained in a good school in the most difficult study of counterpoint, can start on any other kind of composition and handle it correctly,

---

[20] Christoph Bernhard (1627–92) was a pupil of Schuetz from ca. 1647 and served for a time as assistant conductor of the Dresden court orchestra in the reorganization following Schuetz's retirement. The Elector twice sent Bernhard to Italy to study. He later joined Matthias Weckmann in Hamburg after intrigue by the Italians at the court had forced him to leave.

[21] Matthias Weckmann (1618–74) sang under Schuetz in the choir at Dresden and later studied under him. The Elector provided support for Weckmann's studies under Michael Praetorius in Hamburg. Weckmann returned in 1641 as organist at the court chapel and was officially appointed co-director in 1648. He later moved to Hamburg.

[22] Johann Theile (1646–1724), a composer, singer, and viol player, studied under Schuetz in his retirement. Theile moved to North Germany and composed a *Singspiel* for the opening of the Hamburg opera house in 1678. In later life he returned to Saxony.

[23] Christoph Bernhard's *Tractatus* was circulated widely in Germany, though never published until 1926, when it appeared under the title *The Composition Method of Heinrich Schuetz in the Version of His Pupil Christoph Bernhard*. Bruno Grusnick has challenged this contention in his article on Bernhard in *Die Musik in Geschichte und Gegenwart*. It is the current consensus that Bernhard's *Tractatus* more likely reflects the methods of Zarlino, Scacchi, and Carissimi, as well as Schuetz.

unless he has first trained himself sufficiently in the style without *basso continuo* and has also mastered all the prerequisites for regular composition, such as: disposition of the modes; simple, mixed and inverted fugues; double counterpoint; different styles for different kinds of music; part-writing; connection of themes, and so on, of which the learned theoreticians write profusely and in which students of counterpoint are being orally trained in technical schools. No composition of even an experienced composer lacking such a background (even though it may appear as heavenly harmony to ears not properly trained in music) can stand up or be judged better than an empty shell.[24]

While his use of the chorale was not as all-embracing as, for example, Praetorius, Schuetz made use of both chorale texts and melodies in a variety of ways.[25] There was also no question about his allegiance to Martin Luther's cause, as his high praise for Luther's chorale melodies—retained in his *Becker Psalter*—clearly reflects and as his refusal to accept invitations to serve at Catholic courts, even though he was assured the freedom of his own confession, demonstrates.

Schuetz's accomplishments have been summed up in many ways by a variety of scholars. Representative of these assessments is that of one of the great musicologists of the 20th century.

Schuetz was not only the greatest German musician of his period but one of the outstanding creative geniuses in musical history. . . . His sense of form and his musical technique, trained in the classical traditions of polyphony, his earnest biblical faith, and his universal culture effectively protected him from falling victim to mere exterior effects. Although familiar with every secret of contemporary Italian music—dissonance, sharp eruptive modulations, chromaticism, *coro spezzati*, echo effects, dramatic recitation, and instrumental illustration—these are never conspicuous and are always subordinated to higher artistic aims. His artistic development shows a steady growth toward simplification and crystallization. All the foreign elements are melted into an epoch-making synthesis in the spirit of German Protestant church music.[26]

It may seem strange that while he was honored in his own time and country as the greatest master, outside of Germany—with few exceptions—Schuetz was scarcely known, his legacy soon forgotten after his death. The time was one which had little sense of history, a time in which

---

[24] See Mueller, op. cit., 192; English translation in Morgenstern, op. cit., 30.

[25] See, for example, Schuetz's *Musikalische Exequien* and the *Becker Psalter.*

[26] Lang, op. cit., 397–98.

the musical needs of the day were provided for according to the prevailing taste. In Moser's words:

> . . . the world around him had undergone great change and he, whose ideals were largely rooted in the Renaissance concepts of the sixteenth century, had already long felt himself out of place and isolated in a musical world which was already succumbing to the influence of Lully.[27]

In the years following his death, Schuetz was overshadowed by the generation of Buxtehude, Pachelbel, and Boehm, and—more dramatically—by the achievements of Bach, Handel, and Telemann. The recovery of the Schuetz legacy, begun in the 19th century, was effected through the various efforts of such men as Winterfeld, Brahms, Liszt, Chrysander, Spitta, and Arnold Mendelssohn. Building on these efforts, the work of a variety of 20th-century scholars, composers (notably Hugo Distler), and performers have resulted in a renewed understanding and appreciation of the insights and work of this musical giant of the 17th century. Schuetz was one of the church's major musical prophets and must be counted among the greatest composers of all times.

[27] Moser, *Heinrich Schuetz: A Short Account*, op. cit., 98.

1580 1590 1600 1610 1620 1630 1640 1650 1660 1670

HEINRICH SCHUETZ

Historia der . . . Auferstehung . . . Jesu Christi

Italian Madrigals (1611/12)

Psalmen Davids (1619)

Cantiones sacrae (1623)

Becker Psalter (1628)

Symphoniae sacrae I (1629)

Musikalische Exequien (1636)

Kleine geistliche Konzerte (1636/39)

Die sieben Worte Jesu Christi am Kreuz (1647)

Symphonia sacrae II (1647)

Geistliche Chormusik (1648)

Symphonia sacrae III (1650)

Zwoelf geistliche Gesaenge (1657)

Historia der Geburt Jesu Christi (1664)

Passions (1665/66)

Guide to Heinrich Schuetz's Collected Works

Schuetz, Heinrich. *Neue Ausgabe saemtliche Werke* (*NSA*). Currently 40 vols. Kassel u. Basel: Baerenreiter Verlag, 1955—.[28] (In progress).

The following works are listed in chronological order.

1611/12   *Italian Madrigals* (*NSA* 22)
            Revised and translated by Hans Joachim Moser. Preface in English translation. Nineteen secular pieces with Italian texts set for voices without *basso continuo*. Eighteen in five parts, one in eight parts, double choir.

1619   *Psalmen Davids* (*NSA* 23, 24, 25, 26)
            Edited by Wilhelm Ehmann and Werner Breig. Preface in English translation. Collection of 26 large-scale polychoral works for two to four choirs with *basso continuo*.

1623   *Historia der . . . Auferstehung . . . Jesu Christi* (*NSA* 3)
            Edited by Walter Simon Huber. A resurrection oratorio for solo voices, choir, instruments, with *basso continuo*. Opening and closing choruses, solo voices, and instruments in the middle section.

1625   *Cantiones sacrae* (*NSA* 8, 9)
            Edited by Gottfried Grote. Preface in English translation. Forty Latin motets in four parts with *basso continuo*, mostly written in the older polyphonic style. Texts from the psalms and the prayer book of Andreas Musculus. Includes five table graces.

1628   *Becker Psalter* (*NSA* 6, 40)
            Edited by Walter Blankenburg. Cantional-style settings in four parts of the metrical psalm paraphrases of Cornelius Becker. Based on Schuetz's enlarged edition of 1661.
            First version 1628. Edited by Werner Breig. Preface in English translation. (See preface to *NSA* 40 for a detailed description of the differences between the 1661 and the 1628 editions.)

---

[28] An earlier edition is Heinrich Schuetz, *Saemtliche Werke* (18 vols.; ed. P. Spitta et. al.; Leipzig: Breitkopf and Haertel, 1885–1927). For an edition just recently begun, see G. Graulich, et. al., eds., *Heinrich Schuetz: Saemtliche Werke* (Stuttgart, 1971—).

1629   *Symphoniae sacrae I* (*NSA* 13, 14)
            Edited by Gerhard Kirchner and Rudolf Gerber. Preface in
            English translation. Twenty settings of Latin texts. Nos. 1–10
            are for two voices with two instruments and *basso continuo*.
            Nos. 11–20 are for one to three voices with two to four instru-
            ments and *basso continuo*.

1636   *Musikalische Exequien* (*NSA* 4)
            Edited by Friedrich Schoeneich. A German requiem written
            for the funeral of Prince Heinrich Posthumus. Part I is written
            as a *Missa brevis*; Part II is a motet for double chorus; Part III
            is a setting of the Nunc Dimittis and a text from Revelation
            for chorus and three solo voices.

1636/39   *Kleine geistliche Konzerte* (*NSA* 10, 11, 12)
            Edited by Wilhelm Ehmann and Hans Hoffmann. Preface
            in English translation. Fifty-five settings in two volumes for
            one to five solo voices with *basso continuo*.

1647   *Die sieben Worte Jesu Christi am Kreuz* (*NSA* 2)
            Edited by Bruno Grusnick. A dramatic oratorio-like setting
            of the Passion story for five-part choir, solo voices, and
            instruments with *basso continuo*.

1647   *Symphoniae sacrae II* (*NSA* 15, 16, 17)
            Edited by Werner Bittinger. Prefaces in English translation
            Twenty-seven settings of German texts. Nos. 1–12 written for
            solo voices with two instruments. Nos. 13–22 written for two
            solo voices with two instruments. Nos. 23–27 written for
            three solo voices with two instruments. All with *basso con-
            tinuo*.

1648   *Geistliche Chormusik* (*NSA* 5)
            Edited by Wilhelm Kamlah. Twenty-nine motets for five to
            seven voices. Four have instrumental accompaniment.
            Feature German texts, and the motets are arranged according
            to the church year.

1650   *Symphonia sacrae III* (*NSA* 18, 19)
            Edited by Werner Breig. Preface in English translation.
            Twenty-one large-scale pieces for three to five voices, some
            with choir and instruments and double chorus.

1657   *Zwoelf geistliche Gesaenge* (*NSA* 7)
            Edited by Konrad Ameln. Preface in English translation.
            Written for four voices, nine pieces are intended for the
            church service (including a Kyrie based on the "Kyrie fons
            bonitatis" and a Gloria based on "All Ehr und Lob"), and the
            remaining three pieces are intended for the school.

1664   *Historia der Geburt Jesu Christi* (*NSA* 1)
            Edited by Friedrich Schoenlich. Large-scale setting of the
            Christmas story for choir, solo voices, and instruments with
            basso continuo.

1665–66   *Passions* (*NSA* 2)
            Edited by Wilhelm Ehmann (*Luke* and *John*) and Fritz
            Schmidt (*Matthew*). The Passions of *Luke, John,* and
            Matthew, probably written in that order. For four-part choir
            with solo voices, unaccompanied.

                            * * * * * * *

Einzelne Psalmen (*NSA* 27, 28)
    Edited by Werner Breig. Preface in English translation.
Twelve settings of psalms not belonging to any collection.
Includes settings for four- and five-part choir and two and
three choirs. Included is a Magnificat for two choirs.

Trauer Musik (*NSA* 31)
    Edited by Werner Breig. Preface in English translation. Six
commemorative motets written at the death of persons close
to Schuetz.

Choralkonzerte und Choralsaetze (*NSA* 32)
    Edited by Werner Breig. Preface in English translation.
Separate compositions based on chorale texts, most of them
also on chorale melodies.

Weltliche Lieder und Madrigale (*NSA* 37)
    Edited by Werner Breig. Preface in English translation.
Fourteen pieces, all with secular texts. Includes songs and
madrigals with and without instruments.

Weltliche Konzerte (*NSA* 38)
   Edited by Werner Bittinger. Preface in English translation. Settings of secular Latin texts for four-part choir or double chorus with instruments.

Der Schwanengesang (*NSA* 39)
   Reconstructed and edited by Wolfram Steude. Preface in English translation. Includes Psalm 119 in 11 parts, plus Psalm 100 and a German Magnificat. For two four-part choirs and *basso continuo*.

Selected References for Further Reading

Primary Sources:
Schuetz, Heinrich. *Neue Ausgabe saemtliche Werke*. Currently 40 vols. Kassel u. Basel: Baerenreiter Verlag, 1955—. (In progress). (Prefaces to the following volumes appear in English translation: vols. 8, 9, 10, 11, 12, 13, 14, 15, 16, 17, 18, 19, 22, 23, 24, 25, 26, 27, 28, 31, 32, 37, 38, 39, and 40.)
Mueller, Erich H., ed. *Heinrich Schuetz: Gesammelte Briefe und Schriften*. Regensburg: Gustav Bosse, 1931.
Spagnoli, Gina, trans. and ed. *Letters and Documents of Heinrich Schütz, 1656–72: An Annotated Translation*. Rochester: University of Rochester Press, 1992.

Secondary Sources:
Gudewill, Kurt, and Werner Bittinger. "Schuetz, Heinrich." Cols. 202–26 in vol. 12 of *Die Musik in Geschichte und Gegenwart*. Kassel u. Basel: Baerenreiter Verlag, 1965.
Heinrich Schuetz and His Times in Pictures. Compiled and commented on by Richard Petzold. Introduction by Dietrich Berke. Kassel: Baerenreiter Verlag, 1972.
Mattfeld, Victor. "The Use of Instruments in the Music of Heinrich Schuetz." *The American Organist* (March 1988): 65–69.
Moser, Hans J. *Heinrich Schuetz. His Life and Work*. Translated by Carl G. Pfatteicher from 2d rev. ed. St. Louis: Concordia, 1959.
———. *Heinrich Schuetz. A Short Account of His Life and Work*. Edited and translated by Derek McCulloch. New York: St. Martin's Press, 1967.
Mudde, Wilhelm. "Heinrich Schuetz: Composer of the Bible." Pages 79–91 in vol. 7 of *The Musical Heritage of the Church*. Edited by Theodore Hoelty-Nickel. St. Louis: Concordia, 1959.

Rifkin, Joshua, and Kurt Gudewill. "Schuetz, Heinrich." Pages 1–37 in vol. 17 of *The New Grove Dictionary of Music and Musicians*. Edited by Stanley Sadie. New York: Macmillan, 1980.

Schrade, Leo. "Heinrich Schuetz and Johann Sebastian Bach in the Protestant Liturgy." Pages 170–90 in vol. 7 of *The Musical Heritage of the Church*. Edited by Theodore Hoelty-Nickel. St. Louis: Concordia, 1959.

Smallman, Basil. *Schütz, The Master Musicians*. Oxford: Oxford University Press, 2000.

Afterword

Much has transpired in the history of church music since the 16th and 17th centuries. Some things have been gained, and perhaps some things have been lost. In a modern culture in which piety is often substituted for craftsmanship, in which an increasingly secularized world tends to isolate "church" music from the main streams of music, in which new musical styles are looked on with suspicion by many as somehow inappropriate for corporate worship, and in which an unrestrained emphasis on the personal and subjective has loosened—and in some cases broken—ties with the historic worship of the church, it is clear that the world of church music today is hardly the same as that encountered by these early church musicians of three and four hundred years ago. Yet simply to say, "That was then, this is now," is to dismiss too easily a tradition from which we have much to learn and which can help us find our way through the problems and challenges of our own day.

There is much in the lives and work of these pioneer musicians in Lutheranism's first century and a half which can be helpful and useful to church musicians and to the church today as it seeks to find a way between mere repristination of what some consider a fossilized past and much of so-called "contemporary" church music which seems frivolous, inconsequential, and lacking any roots in the history, life, and tradition of the Christian church. Let me suggest several characteristics of the lives and work of these men which, it seems to me, have application and implications for our own time. While they apply to each of these men in varying degrees, they are worthy of reflection today as church musicians seek to find their way through a time in which the problems and challenges before us seem so dramatically new, yet on closer examination, are surprisingly old.

All were musicians highly trained in their art and craft. Coming from a wide variety of family backgrounds—Walter was the son of a farmer, Hassler came from a family of musicians, Praetorius and Schein were the sons of pastors, Scheidt was the son of a barkeeper, and Schuetz the son of an innkeeper—they were all recipients of the best musical training and education of their time. Some were schooled in court chapels (Walter, Schein, Schuetz), some were pupils of the most illustrious teachers and composers of the day (Hassler, Scheidt, Schuetz). But whatever their particular background, each saw himself as a musician for whom the best and most proper exercise of his piety—as a musician—was possible only by exercising the highest degree of craftsmanship and skill of which he was capable.

Today many churches are afflicted by musicians, many of them well-meaning and occupying positions of influence, who are not only lacking basic musical skills, but who flaunt their inadequacy of training as affording a more direct path to greater sincerity and self-expression. Such an attitude would not only be puzzling to these early Lutheran church musicians; congregations who sought in their musical leadership only the very best would not have tolerated it.

All were musicians involved, in varying degrees, in the secular musical life of their day. While to some extent this was the result of the musical needs of their patrons or the conditions of their employment, it reflected as well the broader outlook of the Christian humanism of the time. One need only look at the secular madrigal collections of Hassler or Schuetz, the student songs of Schein, the instrumental dance collections of Praetorius and Schein, Schuetz's first German opera or his festival *masques* (scores of which have unfortunately been lost), or the various works for birthdays or other festivities for which most of these composers were obliged to provide. All reflect an outlook which extends beyond what today is usually seen as the vocation of the "church musician" and which saw all of music—as part of God's creation—as a gift for humanity's enjoyment and delight as well as being a vehicle for the expression of profound religious sentiments.

Today most church musicians are embarrassingly unaware of the world of serious secular music. Most attend few concerts; fewer are acquainted with the serious music and musicians of our day. Yet it was just such involvement and acquaintance with the world of serious secular music on the part of these early Lutheran church musicians and composers that provided the impetus for the musical changes from the "old style" to the "new" described in the preceding pages. In the first century and a half of Lutheran music, to be concerned with "contemporary" meant to be immersed in the serious new advances in music emanating from Italy. Today, to be interested in "contemporary church music" means to be involved with the least significant, most frivolous, and most ephemeral music of the popular culture in pursuit of a kind of "outreach" or "evangelism" which largely misunderstands the nature of both outreach and evangelism.

All—with the exception of Johann Walter and Georg Rhau—*were musicians who wrestled in various ways with the challenges and implications of a "new" musical style for the church.* Their solution, simply stated, was to cautiously experiment with the new without rejecting the old. Each of these composers from Hassler to Schuetz used, to varying degrees, both the old and new styles. While Lutheran theologians were fulminating against the new "concertizing" style, these musicians continued to explore and develop the possibilities of the "new" in ways which were to give freer course to the "preaching" of the Word through music. They did this not by turning their backs on the tradition they had inherited—indeed, they continued to promote, encourage, and nourish it—but rather by building toward the future on the basis of that tradition. And the pivotal point, which kept these two aspects in balance, was the chorale. It was the chorale melodies which, for the most part, furnished the musical material for their forays into the new and which gave the listener a point of contact with the familiar. It is of interest, parenthetically, to note that the greatest contributions of these men to the future course of church music is to be found precisely in those aspects of their work in which they pressed beyond the boundaries of the "old."

All were musicians who found the liturgy and the worship of God's people to be the most natural and appropriate context for the greater part of their music. Whether one looks to the succession of cantional collections, the chorale-based material, the Scripture-based motets, or the larger and smaller concerted works, it was the proclamation of the Word in the liturgy and in the variety of other devotional exercises in court, school, and church to which their music was devoted. It should also be noted in passing that the significantly large number of works with Latin texts reflects a worship practice in which the Latin language did not give way to the vernacular as quickly or as completely as some have imagined. But whether it was an older style or a newer one, whether the language was Latin or the vernacular, it was the liturgy and its attendant forms which provided the impetus, the texts, and the context for the most significant work of these composers.

Today, many churches are moving away from the celebration of the historic liturgy and the tradition of music birthed by the Reformation. Instead, they are turning to worship practices in which entertainment is the major goal, in which the centrality of Word and Sacrament is increasingly diluted, in which proclamation of the Gospel is readily accommodated to the whims of current cultural movements, in which a bottom-line mentality prevails, and in which the Reformation *solas*, upheld in theory, are increasingly difficult to discover in practice. That such tendencies are not seen as lamentable but are trumpeted as solutions to the contemporary situation says much about current ideas of faithfulness to the church, to tradition, and to the Gospel itself.

All of these musicians were influential as teachers. Their teaching was exercised in both formal and informal ways as several generations of young musicians participated in music-making in the court and chapel choirs and in learning the skills of composition from these men. Johann Walter's influence, for example, was perhaps greatest through his influence on those who sang under his direction at Torgau, where his choir at various times included one of Martin Luther's sons, the fathers of Leonhard Schroeter and Michael Praetorius, and Georg Otto, teacher of Heinrich Schuetz. A host of lesser-known names can be cited as evidence of the extent of the influence of these men on a coming generation of musicians. Occasionally one or another pupil rises to a position of greater importance, but for the most part the names of most of these pupils are little known. At various times such young musicians as David Haiden, Georg Dorsch, Erasmas Baumann, and Lukas Behaim came under the influence of Hassler. Scheidt's pupils included Gottfried Amling, Moritz Belitz, Philipp Caden, Zacharias Eckhardt, Adam Krieger, Sebastian Mueller, Gottfried and Christian Scheidt, Georg Vintzius, Daniel Weixner, the brothers Johann and Caspar Ploetz, and possibly Thomas Selle. Schein's pupils included Paul Flemming, Christoph Schultze, Andreas Unger, Christian Knorr, Johannes Kegler, Marcus Dictericus, and Daniel Schade. Among those influenced by Schuetz, either as a member of his choir, as pupils, or as associates, were Christoph Bernhard, Matthias Weckmann, Heinrich Albert, Johann Theile, Adam Krieger, Caspar and Christoph Kittel, Christian Dedekind, Johann Casper Horn, Clemens Thieme, and many others.

In most cases the relation between teacher and pupil meant not only the direction of their musical skills and a concern for their professional advancement through recommendations to suitable positions, but a concern for their personal, material, and spiritual welfare as well. Through such pupils as these and others who were influenced in a variety of ways by these shapers of the early Lutheran tradition, their concerns regarding the church, its liturgy and music, the chorale, and the craft of composition was transmitted to yet another generation of young musicians.

It was to these pupils, then, that the task was given of carrying on the tradition, moving it forward, restating, reinterpreting, and transforming it for their own day. It was a formidable task for both teachers and pupils in the 16th and 17th centuries. It is an equally formidable task for teachers and pupils in our own time.

Appendix A

Comparison of Luther's Orders of Holy Communion
with the *Missale Romanum* of 1570

Missale Romanum (1570)	*Formula Missae* (1523)	*Deudsche Messe* (1526)
Confiteor	(Sermon)	
(Celebrant and Ministers)		
Introit	Introit	Introit
		(Hymn or German Psalm)
Kyrie (ninefold)	Kyrie (ninefold)	Kyrie (threefold)
Gloria in excelsis	Gloria in excelsis	
Salutation and Collect	Collect (one)	Collect
Epistle	Epistle	Epistle
Gradual/Alleluia or Tract	Gradual with Alleluia	German Hymn
Gospel (with Acclamations)	Gospel	Gospel
	Nicene Creed	Creed
(Sermon)	(Sermon)	Sermon
		Paraphrase of
		Lord's Prayer
		Admonition to the
		Communicants
Nicene Creed	Preparation of bread	
	and wine	
Offertory	Preface	
Canon	Words of Institution	Words of Institution
	Sanctus	
	Lord's Prayer	
	Pax Domini	
Communion	Communion	Distribution of the
		Elements
	Agnus Dei	
	Proper	
	Communion	
Post-Communion	Post-Communion	
	Collect	Collect
	Benedicamus	
	Domino	
Benediction	Benediction (Aaronic)	Benediction (Aaronic)
Last Gospel		

Appendix B

In Praise of the Noble Art of Music[1]
Johann Walter
Wittenberg 1538

All those engaged in any art
  Will highly praise its every part,
Tell where it came from, trace its rise,
  And laud its virtues to the skies.
Thus I tell, adding to those throngs,
  What art to *Musica* belongs,
Her status, power, the good she brings,
  And from what noble roots she springs.

When our eternal gracious God
  Had fashioned Adam from the sod
To give him joy throughout his life
  In Eden's garden with his wife,
God told him: "Earnestly obey
  What I command you here today:
Eat any fruit from any tree
  That in this garden you may see
Except that tree whose fruit brings in,
  Besides known good, the taste for sin.
I tell you, do not eat of it,
  For when into that fruit you've bit
Against my will, at once will loom
  Your sentence unto death and doom."

Thus God spoke. Then the serpent came
  With honeyed guile to call Eve's name.
The wish to sin in her he woke;
  So from the tree a fruit she broke
And urged the man to eat it too.
  At once they saw God's word come true;
With sinners' eyes they saw as shame
  Their nakedness, once free of blame.

---

[1] *Lob und Preis der loeblichen Kunst Musica* (1538), *SW* 6.

And, knowing that they had transgressed
    The clear command of God the Blest,
They saw that they would have to die
    And in eternal torment lie,
With all gifts since creation's dawn
    And all God's goodnesses withdrawn.

But God's love from eternity
    Had pity on their misery.
He promised them the Woman's Seed
    To save them and their human breed
From sin, from Satan's wicked hands,
    From mighty death's dark fiery bands.
That Seed would their Redeemer be
    And for God's service set them free.
That such unmerited free grace
    (Which God from love for all our race
Had promised in His Word) might be
    Kept fresh in human memory
And move the heart to high delight
    In praising God both day and night—

This is the weightiest reason why
    God music did at once supply.
Then too, since sin acquired at birth
    Would bring to Adam's seed on earth
Much woe and—earth itself now spoiled—
    Small joy in all for which they toiled,
As antidote against that blight,
    To keep man's life from wilting quite,
And also to rejoice the heart,
    God soon supplied sweet music's art:
In Adam's lifetime God revealed
    To Jubal this delightful field
And lent him power to invent
    Both stringed and windblown instrument;
What Jubal taught, his sons taught theirs
    And multitudes became his heirs.

I have just named two reasons why
    God gave us music from on high.

Those reasons teach us we must use
   The gift from heaven as God would choose:
By it let God be glorified;
   Then let it be our help and guide.

Since this high art most certainly
   Was given by God, as all can see,
It outshines others arts in name,
   Nobility, and lasting fame.
For music and theology
   Were given by God concurrently.
The former with its lovely sound
   Was in the latter hidden found.
God let His peace on both arise
   So that each might the other prize.
To closest friendship they have grown;
   They are as loving sisters known.
When God's Word lives in human heart,
   One finds there harmony's sweet art
In which there is the Spirit's love,
   The proof it came from God above.
No other arts with it compare,
   For it breathes purest Gospel air,
Exalting Holy Writ on high
   And earning highest praise thereby.

Pursuit of it was diligent
   Throughout the older testament,
Whose kings and prophets proved it true
   That men gave music then its due.
It is a wonder truly great
   Beyond what words can estimate
To see what good from music flows,
   And how its hidden power flows.
That you may know this to be true
   Some Scripture proofs I offer you:
When Israel crossed the Sea dry shod
   And Egypt's host was drowned by God,
Then joy from all the rescued throng
   Resounded in a victory song.
As young and old their praises voiced

And in God's mighty arm rejoiced.
God's Law came down on Sinai
　With thundercloud and trumpet cry.
The Jericho walls came crashing down
　When music's power struck the town.

We also read of Gideon,
　God's warrior fighting Midian.
With war cries and with trumpets' blast
　The Midianite foe was set aghast.
In sudden fear they woke confused
　And each against his fellow used
The sword till thousands slaughtered lay
　And Gideon's three hundred won the day.

Observing that their king's sick mind
　An evil spirit had entwined,
Saul's men said, "Someone play and sing
　To calm the madness of the king!"
So David with his harp was brought.
　His playing instant wonders wrought,
For when Saul heard the music play,
　The evil spirit fled away.

Elisha, faithful, did comply
　To royal pleas to prophesy,
But minstrel music first he heard.
　His soul thus calmed, there came God's Word
To him just at the music's height
　To fill his words with Spirit's might.
In Scripture it's quite commonplace
　That prophets' music oft embrace.
It's therefore proper, good, and right
　To show it in a splendid light.

When David came to royal power,
　He brought the art to fullest flower.
Thus many kinds of music mark
　The progress of the golden ark:
First human voice, then dulcet lute,
　The noble harp, the psaltry, flute,

The pipe, the ram's horn, the cornet,
  The trumpet, cymbal, and timbret.
Their sounds combined to glorify
  And loudly praise the Lord most high.
The king's exuberance found a chance
  To praise God even in a dance.
As he before the ark leaped high,
  His wife looked on with jaundiced eye.
Yet David never ceased to strive
  For worship joyfully alive:
See, out of his own means he hires
  Fine instrumentalists and choirs.
Such things have favor in God's sight,
  For His Word notes them with delight.

Worship's praise and music's sound
  Are in the Psalms together bound.
There "songs" and "organs" "praise the Lord,"
  There "players on instruments" "bless the Lord."
The psalmists everywhere proclaim:
  "Sing to the Lord" and "bless His name."
The Psalter builds a noble fort
  For music and its strong support.
Song gives the psalms their richest voice—
  Firm bond in which we all rejoice.
The two in one scale are together;
  You can't weigh one without the other.

Were David here to see fulfilled
  All God had promised, all He willed,
He'd lavish gifts with all his heart
  To increase the musician's art.
May his example be the light
  To guide our leaders to do right,
To love and favor, while they live,
  What sacred music has to give.
Whatever insight they can get
  Into this art they'll not regret.
Who sacred music keeps alive
  Helps many lovely virtues thrive.
It once was rulers' highest praise

That they sincerely tried to raise
The art of music to a height
  By means of their own wealth and might.
Thus formerly the art was prized
  Which now, alas, is much despised.
Wise Sirach's book lets music shine,
  At banquets where there is good wine,
Like sparkling jewels set in gold.
  Search Scripture, find like tributes told.

New testament reveals the muse
  Of music honored in its use.
Thus when our Savior-King was born
  To save us sinners all forlorn,
A sudden glory filled the night,
  And angels from the realms of light
To startled shepherds sang their joy
  And praised God for the newborn boy:
"To God all glory for the birth
  Of Christ who brings peace down to earth.
Proclaim the tidings though the world,
  Let joyful praises be unfurled."
If Scripture never once again
  Praised music with inspired pen,
Yet music's art is amply praised
  By that one song the angels raised.

God for His Gospel oft employs
  The art of music's joyful noise.
The Apostles teach with clarity
  What music's use and goal should be.
By singing psalms and hymns and songs
  God's people should do what belongs
To glad instruction of each other
  Or admonition of a brother.
What's taught by song and harmony
  Must flow from true sincerity.
We must teach well our lips the art
  Of praising God with faithful heart.
Does music not accompany
  God's Word and prayer and liturgy?

What gift most pleases God above?
  Our praise that glories in His love.

More room than here I dare to make
  Those many witnesses would take
Who testify how men have sought
  The art by which great song is wrought.
No other art on earth compares
  With sounding forth celestial airs.
It quells emotions that annoy
  And opens wide the springs of joy.
It lifts the heart to rise for prayer
  And with rejoicing fills the air.
It tunes the spirit to the chord
  That bonds faith to the living Word.
The warrior's courage it inspires,
  Beasts hush to listen to its lyres,
The war steed hears the trumpets sound
  And paws impatiently the ground.
It is not toil of any type
  To lead lambs with a shepherd's pipe.
Oft music's power can defeat
  A raging anger's rising heat.
There's health in music; it contains
  The therapy for ills and pains.
The birds beneath the sky all sing
  As purely as the brightest spring.
When birds make music with delight,
  It lifts one's wonder to a height
How music's art supplies the notes
  That issue from birds' throbbing throats.
God placed within all living things
  A glad response when music sings.
A man by music never moved
  Himself a stick or stone has proved.
Yet this comparison's too mild;
  He's worse than beast out of the wild!

I'll shut the mouth of any clown
  Who sacred music's art puts down
On grounds there happen to be some

Who bring on it opprobrium:
When has the world not done the same
　With other gifts to spurn God's name
And disobey His holy will
　And go the way of sinners still?
Just so God's precious Word is used,
　So tortured, outraged, and abused.
Therewith some feather error's nest
　Or try to cloak sin manifest.
Nor Bible, music bear the blame
　When used by some to their own shame.
All those who quarrel with this art
　Are lame of brain and hard of heart.
But those who love to hear God's Word
　Love also to have music heard.

When God made throat and mouth and tongue
　And for a bellows gave the lung,
Not aimlessly but by design
　He for His praise did them combine,
Where music's art is dimly viewed,
　The mind must be innately ruse.
Who holds back honor from this art,
　In other gifts should have no part.

Long speeches may bring on a doze,
　So here's my summary and close:
Music stands in high esteem
　As godly art with noble theme.
Music ever walks with God
　Surpassing all the arts that plod.
In heaven alone it's rightly weighed
　When in the judgment scale it's laid.
Cramped here below in husks and shells,
　Unmuffled there like steeple bells.
No further need in heaven to harp
　On grammar fine and logic sharp;
Geometry, astronomy,
　Law, medicine, philosophy,
All doused, and even rhetoric,
　While music beams from candlestick.

"Herr Kantor" every saint will be
  And shine as music's devotee.
Full choirs with utter joy will raise
  To endless heights God's laud and praise
For His infinities of grace
  That shone on them from Jesus' face.
An ever new song they will sing
  To praise the mercies of their King,
St. John says it will never cease,
  This song of victory and peace.
May we be there with God and find
  Ourselves united heart and mind,
Rejoicing with the saints in white,
  The kingdom's chosen sons of light.
Thanksgiving, honor, worship, praise,
  Dominion, glory all the days
Of vast eternity shall rise.
  So let us with the throngs that prize
God's mercies, join the victory shout
  And gird with song the world about
In glorifying God's great name
  Through all eternity the same.
Amen, Amen, so shall it be.
  God grant it both to you and me.
                    (translated F. Samuel Janzow, 1983)

Lady Music Speaks
Martin Luther

Of all the pleasures, joys, and mirth
  There is no finer on the earth
Than sound of woodwind or of string
  Or of the voice with which I sing.
No ill mood can be present where
  A group with singing fills the air.
For anger, hatred, envy, strife,
  Downheartedness, and cares of life
Flee from the sound of joyous song
  And take attendant ills along.
The great good news has set men free

From fear that song a sin might be.
Indeed, its joys please God much more
    Than others in life's ample store.
My singing shatters Satan's works
    And slays the dragon where he lurks.
Observe young David often wring
    From Saul the evil spirit's sting;
He plucked the harp to dulcet tone
    Till murder from Saul's mind had flown.
Let music's calming voice be heard
    That hearts attend God's truth and Word.
When harp was played and music woke
    The Spirit through Elisha spoke.
My best time of the year is spring,
    When birds their joyous carols sing
And both the earth and sky abound
    In their melodious gladsome sound,
Especially the nightingales,
    Whose lovely singing never fails
To all a gladness to impart,
    Which wins man's gratitude of heart.
Much more praiseworthy's the Creator
    Who thus so wonderously made her
To be a songster without peer,
    Skilled to trained musician's ear.
Listen how both day and night
    She sings God's praises with delight.
To Him my song I also raise
    In endless honor, laud, and praise.
                    (translated F. Samuel Janzow, 1983)

Index

DATE DUE
